THE RELUCTANT MARKETER

(Book 1: Live)

SPIRITUAL WISDOM TO CHANGE YOUR MIND AND GROW YOUR BUSINESS

LINDA BASSO

Printed in the United States of America

Published by Author Academy Elite
P.O. Box 43, Powell, OH 43035

www.AuthorAcademyElite.com

Paperback ISBN-13: 978-1-64085-421-5
Hardback ISBN-13: 978-1-64085-422-2

Library of Congress Control Number: 2018955816

Dedication

For those who boldly embrace new ways of working that deeply align with who they are and who they are meant to be. And my grandmother, the first and most influential entrepreneur in my life—thank you for being courageous in your life so I can be in mine.

CONTENTS

1

IN THE BEGINNING

*Imagine moving through your day with ease, grace, gratitude,
and awe. It is possible, we assure you. – channeled wisdom*

The title of this book carries a powerful promise. Change
your reluctant mind and grow your business. This
is offered with great love and respect, though, not
to imply that any resistance you feel is only in your head.
For we all carry some level of reluctance when it comes to
marketing. Some of us feel it often and intensely. Others
only occasionally as they mostly market their businesses with
ease but sometimes feel a bit of dread about this or that task.
Many of us tend to feel reluctant when asked to step into a
new level of visibility: when we want to grow our business
or step into new services or products but aren't sure if it will
work. Even hugely successful entrepreneurs often are still
reluctant to grow into some areas. I know because I've met
them. But here's the difference between those who fail and

those who succeed—success comes from finding the tools to move forward anyway, reluctant or not.

Many of us long for a way to overcome our dragging feet in a way that feels kind, loving, and wants all of us to come along. Times have changed from United States' origins of tough settlers and bootstrap pulling. We shy away from moving forward in a pushy way and say to ourselves—so what if we don't always like sharing what we do with others? We love our work and we are content with the contribution we're making. But in our heart of hearts, we would like to find a way forward—if it's not pushy or tamps down on some part of ourselves. We're sensitive creatures after all.

We've tried the carrot or the stick approach. Believe me, it's not just you. I've chased many desires and ran from many a pain. Along the way, I discovered a startling truth. Change comes fastest, and lasts longest, with grace.

One thing I've come to know very well in the work I do with many entrepreneurs is that if your business isn't where you want it to be, there's something that needs to change. We often think it's something outside of us. If we could just slow down, get that client to sign-up or master that new skill, then we could soar. Or we focus inward, on what we believe we lack inside. If we could just be more confident or worthy, then we could finally have it all.

This book is not filled with pushy strategies or lofty affirmations to change you.

Though following the practices and advice will lead you forward and support you in feeling ease more than reluctance; it will do so holistically. Not only in the outer—leaving you feeling like a fraud on the inside—nor on only the inner—pushing off your success until you're better. The journey of partnering with divine grace gives you the whole package.

Could it be this simple?

Call it spiritual marketing, marketing with the divine, marketing with spirit, or any version of your own; these are all names for the growing movement of bringing our whole selves to our business. These are all names for the art of calling upon spirit or the divine, to assist and support you in your marketing. Yes, it's this simple and is available to all.

This book will uplift your thinking around spirituality in business. For indeed, the time to bring spirit into your business is now. For too long, we have separated our work and our personal spiritual practices. For entrepreneurs especially, this is important because your whole person is involved in your work and you spend much of the day by yourself. Having rituals to ground your day, a relationship with the divine to guide you, and the courage and devotion to attend to your spiritual nature as you move through the day is a must. It is no longer a luxury.

Attending to your spiritual nature as you move through your day is as necessary as breathing.

We all have some slice of the spiritual in us. Our divinity makes us unique, like fingerprints. It's similar to the amazement you feel when you witness a birth or the magic you imagine when you contemplate the stars so far away. It is your own personal slice of awe and is magnificent.

When we were little, we used to say, "Look at me!" as we tried something new, naturally sensing how special we were. Our parents—or grandparents or whatever well-meaning but misguided adults were around us—told us to tone it down and not express ourselves so brightly out of fear that we would be hurt. Seeing us stand so proudly in our unique selves stirred up their fears that being different might lead to rejection, and we quickly learned from them to tone it down.

The irony is it hurts worse to hide our light more than you can imagine. Think of a bolt of lightning locked in a small metal box with no outlet for its magnificent shine. That's you, hiding your light. The task of spiritual marketing is for you to rub the genie's lamp. Not only to get the genie to come out but also to make the lamp shine. It's okay if others are drawn to it or want its power. Because you *are* special. For anyone on the self-growth path, bringing together your spirituality and work is a powerful goal.

Why put the spiritual in marketing?

Marketing is a hot topic, partly because it comes with its own built-in hype. To stay relevant, those in marketing are always promoting, so there is an endless stream of best practices, new tips, tricks, and tools being explained, shared, and hyped up. Marketers are, after all, good at marketing.

It's not all hype. Marketing is crucial to a thriving business. Although selling and delivering the actual product or service may seem more critical to a business surviving, marketing is the gatekeeper that lets the business sell and deliver in the first place. In reality, marketing is woven into nearly every aspect of a business. Marketing starts at the beginning with research to see if there is a market for a product or service. From there, it moves to the creation of the product itself, then on to how to price, promote, and distribute—including branding, packaging, and delivery—along with customer care and repeat business. Even warranty and returns are under the review of marketing! Literally, everything involved with any aspect of the business that touches the customer is driven by marketing.

Marketing also drives several intangibles, like brand awareness, cause and community building, and environmental choices the company makes. Think of marketing as the actual threads that weave the fabric of your business. No wonder there's a lot of attention and pressure around it.

Marketing is woven in nearly every aspect of your business. You'll be most successful if you can learn to love it.

For entrepreneurs, especially purpose-driven ones like me, marketing can be particularly difficult. Our products and services are often personal. They flow from something we are passionate about or are crafted by our own hands. In some ways, we are our business, or at least the separation between us and our business is very thin. We are good at what we do and want to use our talents to make a difference to the world we are part of.

For most, marketing is not the business they are engaged in. Marketing and sales are additional skills they need to garner on top of mastering the product or service they offer. So, reluctance rears its head. In other words, your craft may be well-suited to your introverted state or your passion for detail, while your marketing may ask for the opposite skill set. It's a lot to ask of one person.

Step outside your comfort zone

I'm suggesting an alternative approach. Marketing is really a state of mind. It's not a long to-do list, never-ending campaigns, or endless copywriting and social media. It's an all-embracing approach to achieve visibility for you and your business. Simply stated, marketing is a willingness to connect with other people. Your mind and body state have everything to do with that.

Many people make themselves crazy as they hunch over a computer looking for the things they should do to market themselves when they really need to stretch themselves, head out of the house to meet people, and see what life brings them. They cannot effectively market while hunched over a computer or sitting with arms crossed stiffly, demanding that business come to them. Marketing, more than anything, is an attitude and openness to life.

Now wait, you're thinking, what about those online marketing people who earn seven figures all from their laptop? I want to do that! Here's a little secret—most seven-figure business people are highly visible in their industry and are often out speaking at conferences and meeting people who can move their businesses forward. A tiny sliver of folks (in the .001%) may truly live in their cave of isolation and make money, but odds are it won't be either you or me.

If you think you can't get clients or work done by being out in the world, please reconsider. One of my favorite clients, Nancy, caught my attention at a newly formed women's business meeting I attended as a favor to its organizer. There were only seven of us there and we listened to a speaker for most of the meeting. However, Nancy's one-minute introduction at the beginning of the meeting stood out to me so much that after the meeting, I asked her to tell me more about her story. She was struck by my quick understanding of her background and how that connected to the work she was doing now. She hired me one week later to help tell her story in an important proposal. Three years later, she is not only a valued client but a friend and colleague. Another of my clients came to me because I made a nice connection with his wife in the park while pushing our daughters on the swing.

Another day, I found a videographer for an upcoming project I had when I was sitting in the coffee shop writing, rather than staying in my office by myself. A woman sat next to me and told me to please not think that I needed to move but she was going to be interviewed on camera for her Yelp page. She then went to check on her makeup, leaving the videographer and me a moment to connect; we realized we were in similar businesses and could benefit from knowing each other. If you stay isolated, it's like the universe, source,

God, or whatever you happen to call it, is trying to send you the answers to what you are asking for but can't get through. So, get out and be open to receiving that which you've been asking for.

Cultivate success

How do you overcome reluctance and cultivate a body and mind state that support our success in marketing? Here's how reluctance plays out in the average workday: complain often, avoid what feels scary or new, and scowl every time you have no choice but to sit down to write copy or go networking, all the while reminding yourself that it will never work anyway.

Sound familiar? Even though we know it works against us, the negative feelings pop up when we step into our marketing role.

There's good news! This book is designed to help you overcome your reluctance and uplift your thinking around marketing. I'll show you how to invite a practical spirituality to your business to do exactly that. Although the end is worth it, your journey won't be all sunshine and roses. This book may challenge the way you think and present ideas you find difficult to implement, or hard to sustain.

No journey that has great rewards feels easy along the way— but it's always worth it in the end.

Well, welcome to life. What is worth doing that doesn't challenge us, at least at first? Once you accept the challenge, you are on your way to a life within your business that you've only dreamed of. You'll even find the universe will meet you partway, sending you support in the form of people, ideas, and opportunities you could never imagine from where you're standing now. So, get to it; the end result is worth it. As I mentioned at the beginning of this book, you can move through your work day—and your marketing efforts—with ease, grace, gratitude, and awe.

In the chapters ahead, you will learn how to have more grace and be more effective in your marketing. As you become more and more aligned with yourself and with your inner guidance, this will unfold naturally. Things will happen with more ease and less stress.

While much of this work is personal, even a bit unexplainable, I can show you how to explore and discover your own path. I will share steps that have worked for me and my clients to encourage and inspire a merging of our vast human business capacity with the vast divine cosmos. I'll start where I am; you start where you are.

Maybe *you* already see how much you'd benefit from this path. In today's business world, it's clear not all people do. Many spend their weekends seeking a more peaceful stance with their yoga classes and self-help books only to arrive Monday morning in their business to force things ahead, no matter the cost. To call on spirit or the divine means you no longer believe you're alone in your marketing. You understand that at all times, in all places, there is something greater happening around you. And you desire to be part of that.

Why should you change your perspective at work? Well, first of all, for most of us, work is the activity in which we spend most of our waking time—even if we have children, partners, or are active in our communities. Add the hours up and work usually falls to number one or two on the list, neck-and-neck with sleep.

When you want change, look for the one element that's likely to make the biggest impact, the lever that moves the most with the least effort. In this context, work makes the most sense. Not only is it the largest chunk of our wakeful time, it has deep ties to our personal lives, especially since it generally funds those. Not superficially, either. For most of us, the acts of shelter, food, and water are tied to the money we earn with our work. Emotionally, this matters. If our survival is tied to something, and it's not going well, every aspect of our lives is impacted.

For small businesses, marketing is tied to our health and success. It could be the lever that once moved, pushes all the other pieces in our world from inside the business out to our personal lives.

It's not the amount of activity or time that you spend being spiritual at work that counts. It's the overall frame of mind and ongoing cultivation that you do. You could spend an entire day in your garden, but if you left it alone for the rest of the month, that day would be lost in weeds. Instead, tend to your garden, day by day. A little bit of weeding done every day never lets the overgrowth begin in the first place.

Same with work. Your one-day spiritual retreat, although relaxing, may not do much for the rest of your work month. A few small actions taken every day can sustain you for the rest of your career. Don't be fooled by the smallness of the actions you can take. As Mother Teresa said, "Not all of us can do great things. But we can all do small things with great love."

Why me? Meet your guide

Growing up in the Midwest, I was taught not to trust sales people. Used car salesmen were held up as the worst of the worst. In fact, anything to do with sales was considered suspect. Marketing? Way too close.

In college, I chose graphic arts as my major; I felt pleased that I had found a business way of being in art. Then, I thought about the unsavory industry I was getting mixed up in. I vowed to not stay in it too long, as everyone knows that the field of advertising and marketing doesn't contribute any good to the world. Unfortunately, this line of thinking stayed with me throughout the first 20 years of my work life!

Eventually, I moved to San Francisco, where the graphic arts were somewhat revered or at least, slightly cool; I found the flexible, creative nature of the work to fit me well. To vent some of my frustrations, I moved towards the eco-side of the design business, using vendors who had green practices. Later, I let go of clients whose companies weren't making a positive impact and only worked for those who were making a contribution. But I still felt guilty.

I felt I didn't belong. Because I believed that I was doing something unsavory, I never really put my heart into growing my business. I didn't connect with the others in my industry who loved what they were doing. I told myself that I needed the money and had to stay with what I knew in order to earn a living. I was simultaneously supporting and punishing myself.

Sound familiar? Then, you know this is a hard way to live.

Fortunately, early on I discovered personal growth via books and I delved into books by Louise Hay and The Artist's Way. I participated in self-growth courses like the Hoffman Process and body-centered therapy groups. I even became part of an ashram and learned how to meditate and teach yoga. All this was part of a journey that, with lots of twists and turns, led me to write this book.

In a way, I was living two lives. If I'm honest, it was partly driven by my need to fit in. This was deeply ingrained from my childhood. My father had grown up in a financially strapped family that was emotionally unstable. They were good people but they had definite issues. His solution? Bootstrap himself through college and get into business. He left his family of origin and all that it entailed. Did he succeed? Yes, but at the cost of never stepping out of line of what he thought made someone successful—or not. I grew up being told that if I stuck out or was different, I would suffer. So, I tried to fit into his mold.

Few in my professional life knew of my spiritual and personal growth orientation. I pretended my spiritual side didn't matter to my work. In my spiritual circles, I found it hard to admit I was in marketing. Instead, I opted to highlight my artistic nature. I was a graphic designer, not in branding; I was a freelancer, not an owner of a firm. In both worlds, I felt the need to downplay the other so I would be accepted.

In 2014, tired of the split and ready to finally do good with my work, I discovered coaching. I had enough mastery in the marketing world that I earned good money with only part-time hours each week and had time for school. I moved to Sonoma County and tried, once and for all, to quit this field to finally do something that made a difference. I wanted to become a life coach to help others live bigger, fuller lives on their own terms.

In the process, I realized I could make a big difference right where I was. Rather than tossing out my 20+ years of marketing and branding experience, I could combine coaching and marketing to help entrepreneurs have bigger, fuller businesses on their terms. Because the truth is, to grow your business, you need to grow yourself. For this, you need a coach. This allows me to bring all my skills to bear on impacting lives in a significant way.

Grow yourself and you'll grow your business.

But even here, where I seem to be finally in a moment of congruence in my professional and spiritual life, I am being pushed further. Apparently, the journey of being authentic vs. fitting in isn't over. This book clearly makes my beliefs about bringing the spiritual and business together public, which is slightly uncomfortable. What will all my past colleagues think? Probably nothing, of course, but you can see how the inner voice of doubt sneaks in when you step out of the crowd.

Even less comfortable is the way writing this book came about. In October of 2015, I didn't clear space on my calendar with the idea that it was time to write a book. Rather, I started to have an urge to write, which I couldn't ignore. When I sat down to write, it wasn't my own words that sprang to my mind. I don't know quite how to explain it other than to say that when I opened my mind to see what this urge to write had to say, all kinds of words came tumbling through almost faster than I could type them. A little confused but curious, I allowed them to come. The amazing thing was how quickly and consistently they came. I could sit and write a thousand words in about 20 minutes with my eyes closed. My fingers seemed to have a life of their own. Since I had wanted to write a book for as long as I could remember, this felt pretty darn exciting. Books I had read about writing said to aim for a thousand words per day and here I was banging that out in less than half an hour. I did this for about a month and the book was born. Of course, that was only the beginning. It took the next two and a half years to translate and organize these profound but densely packed messages so they could be applied to my—or your—work lives.

This birth was also a little freaky. It brought up an awful lot of questions. I mean, whose voices are these? Am I losing my mind? Why is this happening to me? Even as I sit here trying to write this experience, it's bringing up tears and waves of sorrow. I never wanted to be the eccentric, weird, woo-woo type prophesying on the corner while city folk stream around me pretending I'm not there. I simply want to be a regular, artsy but business savvy type who helps others rock their business. I just want to fit in. But, the lure of writing a book in such an easy way was hard to step away from.

I started to talk back to get some answers. Honestly, I wanted to know if this was safe. All kinds of things I've heard over the years were swirling through my head. On one hand, I knew about channeling and how positive that could be. I don't know a lot about it, mind you, but I have heard the occasional talk by Esther Hicks or Doreen Virtue and feel they offer a lot of good healing energy to the world. I have also read about older indigenous cultures using a middle man to interpret between the unseen realm and the physical. I've also seen bits in religious texts about demonic or ill-intentioned spirits trying to reach people. Not knowing enough about it left me feeling unsure and a little worried about my sanity.

Ironically, I can only get answers to these questions by moving into the open mindset of letting the words come, in other words, channeling their answers. Sometimes they would answer me while I was writing. Other times, I would try to consciously connect during a time I wasn't writing. I also ran into several people in my community who knew enough about channeling to give me some guidance.

**Stop praying for guidance and support,
then freaking out when it comes.**

Long story short, at some point it was undeniable to me that I was indeed channeling some kind of intelligence outside of myself and that it was benevolent in its intention. Any question I posed was answered in a kind, consistent way. When I read back through the material I was typing, the voice was different from anything I could have created and the subject matter was different from any thought I've ever had. There were even jokes in what I was writing, good naturedly teasing me for being so uncomfortable with the process! It was good and moving material. It was also only the beginning of this book.

I asked if the intention was for me to channel every word for the whole book and the answer was—not if I didn't want to. These were concepts for me to play with and share in a way that might touch modern purpose-driven entrepreneurs as a way to support them on their journey. In other words, it was left up to me to make this book accessible to my tribe—and to get it out to the public. So began the relationship that led to me receiving parts of this book, and writing or translating these concepts to you, my reader. I've added my own thoughts, found examples to support the ideas, and researched further when the idea was around an area that wasn't in my expertise.

When my editor recently asked me to add this bit about channeling to the book, I resisted. After all, this pushes me further into the outer limits of the business community. When I checked in with my guides, here's what I received—

Channeling is not something to be scared of; it is a gift. An intelligent connection shared between minds in different parts of the universe—is like a kind of telepathy. It's available to most people and could be a source of great comfort and support. It's not because we are divine beings with some kind of larger intelligence. It's because when you channel, you tap into the larger space that is collective to all beings. And, this feels profoundly settling. When tapped into the larger collective, you realize you are not alone and never could be. There is a source of divine intelligence available to you, at all times. Not that we are giving you specific advice, but that there is a channel on the radio dial, if you will, that you can tune into to receive frequencies from others you share the universe with.

I can live with that. Weird? Yep. Insane? I don't think so. I still feel mixed about this whole thing, mind you. It's not easy to step outside of what's considered normal and OK. All my life I've had a big vision. That's generally how I best help others—when I push the envelope and create a bigger world for us all to live in. It's inspiring when big ideas come our way and change our perspective. So, I hope this book has a big impact on your life—and that you'll let me know what that is.

2

SPIRITUAL MARKETING

You must make a conscious effort to move yourself from your "normal" state to a state in which you are in the flow of divinity. Now, truly it is possible to live in this state always and in all things but most of you do not avail yourself to this possibility and so must make a conscious choice in order to bring about this state. – channeled wisdom

Marketing redefined

These days, marketing isn't straightforward in its definition. Why? Because, it's organic. Marketing—the process or approach a business takes to become visible to potential clients, as well as to serve them—changes as often as services, products, and the people creating them change. It fits into the broader context of the society it exists in. It's not static because, at a core level, it's about people and their commerce-oriented relationships that flow forward in the same never-ending tide that life does.

Marketing used to be defined narrowly as the promoting and selling of products. That's because it literally came from the original source of commercial exchange: the market. Even as the literal marketplace in each town was replaced by door-to-door and other kinds of sales, the mindset remained that the market was for the products and goods that kept day-to-day life going. No wonder the early days of business—and marketing—were about promoting and selling these goods.

At some point, business began to be about more than the goods we need in our lives. As we crested the century change in the late 1800s, incomes crested with it, providing additional money for goods beyond life's necessities. The industrial tide delivered more affordable, mass-produced goods. Advertising blossomed to both bolster this trend and take advantage of it. The first billboard mechanism was created in 1900 for the waves of auto travelers who could now afford a car and a trip to the department store for conveniences for their homes. Advertising was the main method of marketing for nearly 50 years. Paying to put companies' names in front of consumers was all it took in these early years of sales.

After a while, things began to even out. By 1950, products were so numerous and of such equal quality that paid announcements were no longer enough. That's when the idea of a soft sell came along and products were tied to the emotional benefits people might gain when using the right product. Companies began inventing reasons why their product was different from another. You could gain sales by promoting the intangibles of your product such as safety, quality, and ease. By the 1990s, big companies took this one step further and invented branding to distinguish nearly identical products from one another. Branding gave the company and its products a personality that a consumer could not only relate to but become loyal to. Now companies don't just have products: they have an attitude, an approach, and a philosophy consumers can identify with. Then, came

Internet sales. You can buy anything you need and have it delivered to your door—with free returns—if you don't like it.

The explosion of commerce all these innovations created during this 68-year period boggles the mind. No wonder marketing has that same mind-boggling effect on us. It has kept pace with the most explosive, planet-changing time in our history.

Marketing, based on today's definition, begins in the early stages of penciling out the idea and continues with identifying the market that exists and whether or not the idea continues to be marketable. It doesn't stop there but goes on through to developing the product or service in ways that fit what potential clients want. It flows, too, into customer service, encouraging repeat business—the bloodline for most businesses. Marketing then fosters the brand, or better said, the relationship between the company and its clients.

Earlier, I mentioned that at its most basic, marketing equals being visible to others. Taking that deeper, it's about increasing your ability to serve and correctly inform people so they can make good choices. For a larger company, that's a neutral process. After all, it's not about any one person. In a small business, it's all about us. Becoming visible and making connections can make us feel vulnerable, and the whole process can drive us a little crazy. Especially if we have stress, trauma, or abuse in our background when we likely learned being visible or connecting to others wasn't always safe.

At all times, there is something greater happening around you and it can support your efforts if you let it.

Marketing as a profound act of service

Are you a purpose-driven entrepreneur? Do you believe your product or service somehow contributes to the greater good of others or the planet?

As a marketing coach, I work with small business owners like you. They are not all environmentalists or healers, though some are. They often run regular types of businesses like hair salons, dance studios, or bookkeeping firms. What they have in common is a deep desire to express themselves authentically and from a sense of purpose.

Don't worry if you can't articulate this fully. They can't either but they are living it! They sense that they've been called to their work or see that by doing their work, they are making a unique contribution to their clients. They often admit that many others are probably offering their service in ways that may sound better or more profitable, but they hold that knowledge alongside the belief that they are offering what they can, in a way that is special to them.

They believe the work they are doing is making the world better, too. In small ways, like making their clients' day easier or helping their clients accomplish something. Or, in big ways, when they help their client do something like meet a lifelong goal, impact the environment in better ways, or be of service to thousands of others. When questioned about this, they flash a sheepish grin and get a *pinch me, I can't believe this is real* look on their faces.

Usually, they have arrived at their present stage in their business with what they believe to be little or no marketing. It's all been word of mouth or one thing leading to another. They often don't believe they have much in the way of marketing skills. They come to me because they've reached a place where they believe they have to do "real" marketing in order to keep it going or to grow it. Sometimes they have some marketing savvy or have done a lot of marketing but haven't really enjoyed it, either because the system they've followed doesn't feel authentic to them or because they've been believing that the marketing is keeping them from their real work.

Growth is a constant in their world. Just as they reach one stage in life, other stages begin to unfold. The words—it's always something—are heard often in their business circles or at dinner with friends. This is true in either their personal life, their business, or both. Often, they are personally growing at a rapid rate to keep up with all this change. They flip between being exhilarated and exhausted. It's no wonder they question what they're doing, right and wrong.

I, too, am one of these purpose-driven entrepreneurs. As I continue to grow myself and my business, I continue to step into emergent spaces. My most recent was a particularly big one when I realized marketing and spirituality go hand in hand. In having the courage to step into this new space, I discovered a powerful truth: marketing, when done well, is a profound act of service.

I've been using this phrase in all my talks in the last year. Generally, when I say it, the room gets a little quieter. There's a moment of reflection as the possible importance of this phrase sinks in. People who came to figure out their marketing —what they're doing right, what they're doing wrong, what could be better—take a breath. They heave a tiny sigh of relief when they hear this. Why? Because it touches on the deeper level of why they are trying to figure out their marketing in the first place. Every solopreneur and small business owner I know is trying to figure out their marketing so they can make a greater contribution.

They've been thinking marketing is a necessary evil to be done first *before* they can make their contribution. They are relieved by the good news that their marketing—which takes up a lot of their time—is part of the contribution.

It is a profound act of service to do your marketing well.

Now, let's take this even deeper.

Your business *becomes* a profound service when you invite the divine into it. I'm a very practical person. I'm a marketing coach and I'm always taking big ideas or inspirations, and trying to figure out how they can be used. I like ideas, but I like them more when they are in action.

I'm not talking about setting some intention or getting a blessing on your marketing and you are all set (Though I love intentions and blessings!) I'm talking about a practical approach to bring the divine into your marketing at all levels and living it. I'm talking about truly marketing with spirit.

Six benefits of spiritual marketing

It's hard to be spiritual in these modern times. To have an ongoing spiritual practice that takes any substantial amount of time can feel overwhelming when you also must work, socialize, exercise, raise little ones, cook, clean, and all the other things our secular society demands of you. Your spiritual practice need not be something you do separately for an hour a day. This book is all about how to incorporate a spiritual approach to all those things as you go about your daily life.

1. I've chosen to start with spiritual marketing because most people do not like to do marketing, and it brings about a lot of angst—even though it is a lifeline for your business. For entrepreneurs, this is especially important because your whole person is involved in your work and you spend much of the day by yourself. So, having rituals to ground your day, a relationship with the divine to guide you, and the courage and devotion to attend to your spiritual nature as you move through the day is essential to achieving those feelings of ease and grace. It is no longer a luxury. For you on the self-growth path, merging your work and spirituality is the feather in the cap of your life's work.

It's not all about work satisfaction. Consider these added benefits[1]:

- People who pursue spiritual transcendence, regardless of the type of practice or if through a religion, are seen by other people as being more self-actualized, emotionally balanced, and delighted in living.

- Strong personal devotion is associated with higher levels of optimism, education, and income with less neuroticism, and a 15-20% reduction in risk for depression and substance use/abuse.

- Spirituality in an adult's life is linked to less suffering in life, less depression and substance abuse, higher rates of recovery from physical illness, and a longer lifespan.

- Psychological treatments that include a spiritual component have a 20% improvement in depression and anxiety over treatments that don't.

2. If you are easy and free in your work, you give others permission to be the same way. Your frequency and vibration affect all that is around you. Your permission to imagine outcomes far beyond where you are pulls forward the entire world. Someone thought he could fly and did. Now, everyone flies. Someone thought we should be able to connect to any person via a virtual, online connection and viola, we have the World Wide Web, which has literally changed the face of business. Each of us has the possibility for great amounts of inspiration and yet this is largely left untapped. So, dive into your reservoir of inspiration and live your work with spirit!

3. You generate a lot of love if you do devotional practices and this is what is missing in business today. Most days at work, people don't sail through their day blissed out and filled with love. You likely don't go into meetings with your web designer or copywriter, express shared love and then get things done. But, you could.

4. When you take an action and offer it up to something higher than yourself, you are taken out of your small self—the one that's plagued with fears and doubts (Anyone have any of those?). You go from this small self to a higher state. Imagine filling your days with *that* self.

5. By weaving the practices throughout your day, you have the chance to stay connected with your divinity. This style of devotion, not unlike religions that ask followers to pray multiple times per day, is about anchoring one's day around the divine. This can greatly reduce your stress around marketing. Why? Because marketing is one of those activities fraught with anxiety and uncertainty. If only you could have a divine perspective and see the riches and abundance available to you, you would not mind marketing at all!

6. To be filled up and replenished as you move along means you are always full. So, you are meeting with others or doing your marketing work from a rich place, not a place of lack. From there, all things can be accomplished.

When you call on spirit or the divine in your business, it means you no longer work alone.

Quiet your mind

There is a lot of information in this book. And, more in book two and three on this same subject. Some of it may be very different from what you are expecting. Or, it may poke at your inner insecurities. One thing I suggest is trying to quiet your mind and experience, rather than analyze the material you're reading here. I often suggest the same for my clients in all their marketing endeavors. So, let's dive in and start this practice now. In this way, the ideas in the following pages can begin to work with you in the way it's meant to—divinely.

It's amazing what happens when we quiet our minds. For some, meditation is their path, but that's not the only way to stop the chatter and go deeper within. Take a breath. Shift your consciousness. Tune into nature. These can all help you connect with the subtle flow of consciousness around you. When you do this, you are changing the state of your brain waves, working on all the cells in your body, and you begin to feel how profoundly life-affirming it is.

When you try to take in new information or produce your business materials from the distracted place of your own thoughts, you are vastly limiting their impact. This is because you are pulling on a small amount of energy, namely yourself. When you tune into this larger flow of energy, you are instead channeling divine inspiration that seeks to find a connection in the world. Ironically, this is exactly what you are trying to do with your marketing.

You may already be familiar with this state of flow. Many of you do this when you get really into something and lose track of time or say you don't know where that idea came from. As children, we used to do this more naturally, more frequently, before we grew up and experienced the push on productivity. Mulling something over, or giving it time to gestate, used to be common ways of dealing with issues or problems. But, the ego (and our driven culture) stepped in and demanded you to willfully react to things rather than hand them over to the larger consciousness you are part of. Instead, I encourage you to start your work by shifting from the small you to being part of the larger flow.

Here's an exercise to support you in accessing this flow in your marketing. You may want to record yourself reading it aloud so you can relax into it. Or, if you want to download this meditation as an audio file, go to lindabasso.com/reluctant marketer.

Sit comfortably with your eyes closed. Breathe naturally for several breaths, not forcing your breath to do anything different from what it is doing. Now, imagine your breath coming in from one side of yourself and going out the other. You might imagine the air currents coming toward you from the right, going into your right nostril, circulating through your body and then, out your left nostril to join the air currents on the left side of your body. Stay with this breathing for several minutes.

Now, extend this imagining farther out and see that the air currents coming from your right are actually connected to many things in the world. The objects that it passes over, the other people and animals that it breathes through. You can see this connection as millions of tiny golden threads that weave around and through everything, coming into and through you too. As you breathe out to the left, you send the golden threads on their journey to connect with the world around you. You are part of everything you are surrounded by. You have a place in it, and so does everything else. Sit in this golden web, breathing for several more minutes.

When you do an exercise like this, you are signaling something important and concrete to your mind and body—that you are part of a vast web of interconnection in this world. This prepares you to start noticing the connective energy that is always flowing toward you so you can pull from the larger energy moving through our world. If you are tempted to dismiss this as too simple, please don't. Visualization is used by professional athletes, famous actors, and high-performing leaders and executives to accomplish exactly what they create in their mind's eye. Science allows us to see that our body can't distinguish the difference between something really happening around us or vividly imagined. The body releases the same hormonal and physical shifts in either case. If you want to be tuned into the connections around you, use this powerful tool of visualizing it to bring it to being.

As we'll explore throughout this book, there are many other ways to be divinely inspired.

Spirituality or religion?

What do I mean by spirit or God? I mean *your* version of religion or spirituality. Whether that's a formalized religion, a spiritual practice, or just an openness to something beyond day-to-day interactions. I'm equal opportunity! This applies the same to pagans, tree huggers, crystal lovers, and those who attend synagogue, mass or mosque.

How can we look to formal religions or spiritual approaches to guide our marketing? There is, of course, the obvious answer in the principles each religion or spirituality offers that are meant to guide our lives and can be translated to our business approaches.

If you are a Christian, for instance, you have the Golden Rule of doing to others what you would have them do to you. Translate that to your business and you have a guideline for how to treat customers, vendors and colleagues. Expand that approach to your marketing and you see that behaving in ways you appreciate is a great way to be in your marketing efforts. If you have a laid-back lifestyle, and your version of the golden rule makes you think that you can be laid back in your marketing, think again. When I press my clients to think about other people's marketing style they truly appreciate, they almost always share descriptions like thoughtful, consistent, clear, and proactive. In other words, we often appreciate marketing that is well-timed and brings us what we need, but too often we don't incorporate that same approach into our *own* marketing style. Instead, our marketing focus tends to be self-oriented and lacking compassion. We focus on how we can bring in more clients with the least inconvenience to ourselves. We might even become highly critical of our efforts or of those who don't take advantage of what we offer. Not exactly the Golden Rule!

Or, if you are Spiritual But Not Religious—yes, even this group has a set of beliefs which you can read about in my last chapter—you might learn to be seated in your own sense of goodness as the best means to market yourself. The circumstances you found yourself in—stressful or dysfunctional environment, unskilled parents, abusive people—were responsible for shaping some of your reactions and actions in the world, and it's possible you can now choose differently. You can learn to communicate your marketing messages from the place that there is nothing wrong with or bad about you specifically and share your inherent goodness. Plus, no matter what marketing mistakes you've made, you can make new choices in marketing and you'll get new outcomes.

Another viewpoint comes from Judaism and their practice of Shabbat. Considered one of the highest holy days in their calendar year (and yes, one that happens every week), Jews are asked to set aside one full day per week to step outside the demands of daily life to fully replenish themselves. This is considered a radical act of freedom, celebrating their historical freedom, while also pointing out the freedom we should all claim as modern people. The entrepreneurs of today would be well served by considering such a radical act. How much better could your marketing be if you offered yourself true replenishment regularly rather than constantly pushing forward?

There are endless ways to translate the truths shared in religious and spiritual approaches to our businesses. See the bonus chapter in this book for my initial attempts to do this with some formal religions and spiritualties. Though no one approach can tell us how to behave in every situation, we can draw meaning from these teachings and enact them in our daily life to bring the teachings to life. That can make your marketing feel meaningful indeed.

More similar than different

Does it bother you how easily I say God and then switch to a more spiritual and less Christian perspective? Perhaps you are from a major religion and bristle because I place God in the same sentence with the word *marketing*. Or, it bothers you when I leave the more spiritual and focus on a formal religion. Maybe you are a spiritual person who is not comfortable with certain ideologies and belief sets around the God notion. Or, you are part of a faith that doesn't use the word *God*. These differences run deep but I'm asking you to set aside any judgments that come up. Instead, accept the essence of your belief and make room for another's. That is the only way we can end the division sitting in our hearts between spirituality and religion.

Healing can happen when the division stops.

There was a time early in my self-growth work when I was experiencing tremendous loss and pain around discoveries from my early childhood. As my son grew through his early years, I became aware of things that had or had not happened to me at similar ages. I was also so in love with him and deeply afraid that having such a big love surely meant massive heartbreak would follow. Sitting by the water one day, crying and hurting, I realized how angry I was at the world. I told God in no uncertain terms that if something ever happened to my son, I was done. That all the heartbreak I had incurred in my life was one thing, but that if I ever lost him, I could not bear it. For some reason, an image of God appeared in my mind and to my surprise, it was not a he. The image I saw was an elderly black woman, who was kind and maternal. That started a process of intense healing for me. Realizing that I could embrace whatever version of God that worked for me was an empowering step. Now I know the psychology and the science behind that image and process but at the time, it was just something I lived.

Religions have so many more similarities than differences. The leaders in major religions often demonstrate a complete lack of division in the way they treat others. Jesus, Ghandi, Martin Luther King, Mother Theresa, Dali Lama, Pope Francis—all profound examples of people of faith who act outside the bounds of the texts of their religions. To profess ongoing kindness, consideration, and acceptance of others is in every formal religious text. So, isn't it possible there is a misinterpretation when we perceive an us vs. them in a religion? Is it possible we are overlaying our own competitive and sometimes fearful human perspective when we review the language of these religious texts?

People are ready for unity—to come home, step into their divinity, and meet their maker. Not just within religions. The spiritualties I've come across are often in reaction to the perceived negatives of major religions, while focusing on the same positives of those religions: unity, non-separation, returning to one's home, being in one's highest self. Honestly, there are many more similarities than differences. People are ready to step into these similarities and embrace one another. They want to take the best from each and integrate it into a better whole.

Contrary to what is often preached, I believe all the major world religions support your marketing attempts in some way. It's not just the big religions; most spiritual approaches offer insights, too. Am I saying you need to be spiritual to do your marketing well? Not necessarily. My main goal is to give you permission to build a business that truly supports *you*, and for that, marketing is essential. I meet so many entrepreneurs who are trying to power through their business activities in ways that don't feel good to them, and, as a result, aren't successful. Or if they are, they don't feel as happy about their success as they thought they would. Instead, I'm offering tools and insights to support you in doing your marketing in a slightly different way. So many of you are walking around wanting something but not feeling you should have it. Instead, I want you to feel strong about yourself as a creator and as a part of the creator's plan. That is the role you are invited to step into when you market the business of your heart.

Powering through will never move you as far as the divine can guide you.

Once you review all these practices, I believe you will be able to trust that whatever your beliefs are; they can help guide your marketing with divine wisdom. If you can understand that at all times, in all places, there is something greater happening around you, you can trust this to support your efforts. Truly, you can move to be in solidarity with these forces or you can stay to the side, fixed. Imagine a stone in a stream versus a stick. The stick flows with the water—separate from it but carried along with it. Unless it gets caught or stuck on something (which is a whole other topic!), it continues to flow. A rock in the stream is fixed, and the water either goes around or over the rock. Over time, the rock does get worn down and creates less resistance as it gets smoother and experiences less friction—and for some, this is enough. Some rocks get picked up by the water and move, but not with the ease and grace of the stick. You get the point.

To be a stick with your marketing, you need to make sure your state of being isn't like the rock. You should ask for the divine support you need to carry you along. You can ask in whatever way feels good to you. You can pray. You may take a walk in nature and ask nature, the fairies or forest beings to help you. You can light incense and chant divine words. You may do yoga, meditate, or other energy alignment practices. You can ask the air around you. The point is—you must make a conscious effort to move yourself from your normal state to a state in which you are in the flow of divinity. Many people do not avail themselves of this possibility, even though it's available 24 hours a day. As a result, they lack the ease and flow they could enjoy. At worst, this prevents success. At best, it makes success seem like an awful lot of work. It takes conscious choosing to enter this state—but it is worth the effort in so many ways. I invite you to try it.

3

SEEK TRUTH

"The real opportunity to us is the elevation of your planet. To lift the vibrational frequency to a point where you transcend much of the lower or heavy vibrational experiences you currently have there. This process has been happening for years, but recently, there has been a shift in the energies that make it possible to speed things along exponentially." – channeled wisdom

The truth about truth

It's easy to look at truth as a black-and-white concept—true or not true. However, we repeatedly see, even in science, truth often changes. New evidence comes to light disproving a previously proved theory for example. Facts and statistics can be interpreted to mean one thing—or another. New advancements could change our current understanding. Though we all long for things to be black-and-white to ease our way, life doesn't seem to support this all-or-nothing approach. Instead, we face complexity, unknowns, and many shades of gray as we live along the spectrum between black and white.

We live in a dynamic changing environment where scientific experiments don't always produce repeatable results. Every few years, we hear of former theories proven untrue when new evidence came to light. It's safe to drink coffee; no, it isn't. Babies need to lie on their side to avoid sudden infant death syndrome, or is it their back? Experts with excellent credentials find they are at odds with other experts who have equally impressive credentials. Some experiments have even proven the outcome of the experiment depends on the scientist observing it. This suggests science may only be a snapshot of what we currently believe true in the physical realm.

Truth also seems to be deeply personal. We often say—and experience—that what's true for one person holds false for another. In this light, the idea of a mass culture seems ludicrous. Take diets, for example. For some, eating only slow-cooked meats and vegetables will maintain health. Others swear by raw foods with no animal proteins. Some thrive on low-fat, high-carb diets, while others do just the opposite. I can find a Ph.D. level doctor who has done the research to back up each of these diets, yet one set of evidence contradicts the other.

Pick up a book at the bookstore and look next to it for a book proving the opposite. The same is true for medicine. Yesterday's miracle cure doesn't prove out over time. One patient will have a predictable response to a given medication, another doesn't. Stress washes over each of us individually, causing some to become ill, while others are energized.

From a spiritual perspective, here's the truth about truth. It ranges over time and space to encompass all that is. A situation and its opposite are both true. Depending on the situation, circumstances, and people involved, it plays out in one way now and possibly another in the future. Spiritually, this duality has always been tolerated as what makes the universe whole. We are all good and evil, selfish and generous, honest and dishonest. Sure, it can be about the degree to which we are each, but both are true. They may be considered two representations of a single underlying reality, the underlying reality of non-duality.

Even in science, we begin to see the truth in contradictions. The theories of general relativity and quantum fields are incompatible theories of reality, yet both prove true on their own scale. Things we think are solid, like furniture, are made of moving particles. Black holes draw everything inward, but somehow simultaneously emit radiation out. Rather than being linear, time, it turns out, is a logical progression that speeds up or slows down depending on the frames of references of who's observing. Light can be both a wave and a particle, showing that something can indeed be two places at once. Even the animal kingdom weighs in with the contrarian platypus—which contains genes that match mammal, reptile and bird.

As you can see, contradictions are not as problematic as you may think. Universally, black-and-white thinking almost never works. The same holds true for marketing. Clients come to me sure their marketing is right or wrong. They believe there must be one way to do something and if they could find it, their business would work better than it does. Truth be told, for any one business, there are many ways of doing the marketing, not just one. And which will succeed? That's the magic question and can only be answered in experimenting to find what works for now. And then, looking for a new way when that stops working. In the end, there's no black-and-white answer. Rather, it's all an ongoing process.

Other clients come stressed out because they think the only way to be successful in their marketing means doing things they don't like to do. Here's a surprising truth for them: marketing success is relative. There is no one way to do it, only their unique way. They can hate social media and still find an effective way to use it in their business marketing— or not do it at all. Or, they can hate networking and still be visible enough to garner the confidence of people they meet. And, yes, even introverts can succeed in getting in front of enough potential clients. One has to step out of exclusionary thinking—that introverts can't do x, y or z but rather, that one may be an introvert and can have connective conversations given the right circumstances. Or, that one can hate social media and guide their business into the online world in ways that fit. In the end, success can usually be found in the and, not the or.

Finding your truth, spiritual or not

Finding your truth is powerful. Yet, we avoid looking, afraid of what we will discover. The truth doesn't have to scare, nor ask you to make painful changes. It always sets you free. Your truth fills you with incredible joy as it fills you up with your very nature. Truth has a very high vibration, not bound with inconsistencies or lower emotions like guilt or blame. Your truth does not depend on what others would like for you, nor on their fears for you.

Truth, a subtle and delicate thing, must come through experience, not intellect. You were created to have this experience. That is why it comes so often through spirituality, transformational growth, or physical movement. Recognizing the truth helps you live in congruence with your purpose. When you are cut off from your truth, a part of yourself shuts down, which is very painful. That's what you should be scared of—not the truth itself!

We all have many truths—in relationships, friendships, family, community, health, and work. There's your current truth—and truths that were true for you before. Some are complicated truths, like loving and hating something. Or, deciding to stay, while aching to leave.

Each of us also owns a simple truth. Some call it purpose, others a calling, or vocation. Said plainly, it's what we came here to contribute. This truth lights us up because it is a vibrational match for where we fit in the universe. Our little piece of the puzzle, you could say.

You find it by learning to pay close attention to your inner promptings, desires, urges, and inklings. This may sound difficult, but it's not. Difficult? No. Subtle? Yes. To find your truth, you must become sensitive to your response to the things that come along in your life. You will feel a strong resonance in the presence of your truth. Or, sometimes, a strong conflict. Neutrality means that it doesn't hold much for you. If you feel a deep pull toward something, give yourself the option to pursue it until you know the truth of it for yourself. Likewise, if you are in deep conflict about something and you give the conflict enough attention, an informative bit of truth will emerge.

Luckily, the truth never strays far. Like a small, faithful dog, it follows wherever you go. Sometimes you turn and notice it; other times, you call it to come to you. Occasionally, you shake a stick at it and hope it leaves as you toss the stick far away. Persistently loyal, it waits.

Searching for these threads of truth takes your entire lifetime. So, if you've felt pressure to get there soon, relax. Stick with what's true for you currently. The remaining truths in your life are making their way towards you. Sometimes, you can't know the complete truth yet, as pieces of it are still in process. Your maturity level and life experience play a big part in accessing your truths.

Finding and living your truths contributes to what you came here to do. It adds to the overall collective knowledge of our experience here. God or source desires this from us— to know life through our experience of it. Because source is truth, anytime you discover or feel your truth, you are deeply connecting to this divine energy.

It can get complicated because our truths are often obscured or covered by others hopes and fears for us. Or, we may have had negative reactions to our truth when we were young. It can be scary to step into our truth if we think we will lose love or connection with others because of it.

Fortunately, it's not so important to understand every detail of a truth. Instead, know that seeking and living the truth to the best of your understanding meets your highest purpose. Which is to say, the truth that you came to live. You are unique and have different abilities, intellect, emotional systems, etc., so of course, your understanding of truth will be different from someone else's. More importantly, search for *yours* and sit in the knowledge you are living a very high calling.

Finding and living your truth to the best of your ability is your highest purpose.

Turns out that being truthful in your marketing materials serves you well, too. Not merely telling the truth about your services or product, but your unique truths. In other words, your values. When you profess your beliefs in writing, like in your bio, the about page of your website and your company's mission/employee information, you act like a beacon. People who are like-minded can align with you—sharing your beliefs and your values. This doesn't mean they all have to be the same, but things work best when there's resonance or attraction to the same or compatible beliefs and values. It's similar to days gone by when a trader knew that dealing with the Jesuits meant one thing and the Quakers another. When you're truthful in your marketing materials, you're saying you stand for something and are willing to be transparent.

It means you can share your convictions and your tender emotions about love, life, and forgiveness.

When your truth aligns with the spiritual

Why is it hard to share our truth in our business, especially when it smacks of the spiritual? Well, many of us stopped sharing our unique beliefs because we believed we would be passed over because of it. For years, we've lived under separation of church and state. I respect this principle, maintaining the right for all to choose their way of worship. At the same time, taken to the extreme, it has made our workplaces virtually devoid of spiritual practices—and, too often, principles. Add to that, our scientific age that doesn't take seriously that which can't be proven, and the workplace has suffered with too little compassion, justice, and love.

There was a time in history when expressing your spiritual views could mean persecution. We all grew up learning about the Crusades, the Salem witch trials, and the Irish Republican Army (IRA). These are gruesome truths for young minds to comprehend. What we missed in that history lesson was the fact that the violence was rarely over heartfelt beliefs, but rather, over fervor and favor. The extreme acts all came from someone whose beliefs were radical and extremist, rather than following the spirit of the religion. Or, they didn't come from spiritual beliefs at all but rather, the political power tied to the situation. Today's news? Not so different.

Spirituality and religion have also provided comfort, wisdom, and good advice to millions of folks for hundreds of years. Couldn't it be that similar to human beings, these traditions have some good and some bad? We wouldn't execute a person for having some flaws, and I don't believe we should completely walk away from these traditions either.

Find the traditions and practices that resonate for you. Step beyond how your family practiced. Explore other traditions—like those in the last chapter—to find the one or ones that work for you. If it's not in a formal tradition, find the separate pieces and parts that come together to make your approach whole for you. If it's nature, so be it. If it's a church, fine. If it's just a belief in something greater, go with that. You must embrace your beliefs and feel peaceful inside about them. If you are in a certain religion, but only feel inner conflict and doubt and are not actively engaged in working that out for yourself, you are not gaining the benefit of having that spiritual practice in your life.

You must *be* the beliefs you have, not simply broadcast them. The oak tree is so very much itself, and does not try to be anything other than that. We are the only species who spends time hiding itself from itself and others. Animals only do this under great duress and/or abuse. Finding the tradition or set of practices you want to partake of comes first. Creating peace and acceptance within yourself comes second. Working out whatever inner contradictions you have to create inner peace smooths the way for you to embody the beliefs.

Finding the way to share that publicly comes as the third, and oh-so-vital next step. If you find this difficult, follow the example of the Pope Francis or Dali Lama in being kind to others, yet living within your own religion and what you believe it asks of you. The quest to live your own faith deeply, while having as much tolerance and love for others, can be powerful.

Why should you articulate the intangible? It's not whether you can articulate it, but rather, that you can deeply acknowledge it for yourself, and when needed, share it with others in some way.

I find that my clients often struggle with messaging, failing to put into words the very things making them special. I can sense what makes them special, the people who are around them can sense it, but potential customers who haven't met them yet can't grasp this because the messaging hasn't expressed the intangible spirit of this entrepreneur.

Tell a story and you'll get their attention. Before the written word, it was the only way of keeping the intangible experience alive, from generation to generation. Ditto for marketing—you need stories that create strong messages and share your intangibles.

When your truth contains some difficulties

Transparency is the new buzzword in marketing. We are encouraged to build a personal brand, share our values, and let it all hang out in the name of authenticity. Clients want to know the real deal when it comes to the people and companies they buy from. How transparent should we be? It's one thing for a celebrity or the founder of a once-small but now ginormous company (think Apple or Zappos) to have their philosophy and personal life splashed around. It's okay because they made it. The coolness of their success overshadowed any potential backlash about their beliefs, approach, or path there. The public can be radically accepting of a wide range of beliefs when success is involved.

What if you're not famous and you come with a background littered with difficulty? What if your past has made you stronger, shaped who you are and why you do the work you do—but isn't rosy and easy to explain? I've faced this and worked with many clients who face it, too. I call us survivorpreneurs because we are small business owners who've gone through some tough stuff and made it anyway. Ultimately, I want us to move past surviving to thriving.

When you share your truth, you're being brave, bold, and beautiful in your business.

In claiming our truths, and making them transparent to others, we take an important step to becoming bold, beautiful and brave in our businesses. Yes, there are ways to share your story without over-sharing. You can be transparent about the dysfunction, stress, abuse—or the illness, accident, or mistake—that shaped the entrepreneur you've become. To be clear, I'm not talking about whitewashing any violent belief or one that counters respecting others. I am saying you can bring all of you to your business and message in a way that brings you clients, rather than drives people away. We can let go of the fear that if we share the real us, then no one will want to work with us. We can stop using the mask of what we think we are supposed to be, and hoping it works. Which sadly, it rarely does.

Instead, be brave and admit the ways you've struggled. How your journey, warts and all, has brought you here. Especially in your biography—or about section—of your marketing materials. It will feel weird and ungraceful at first. That's because most of us were taught not to share socially unpleasant topics. Remember the adage that if you don't have something nice to say, not to say anything? Let me assure you that it's nice to share yourself with potential clients, so they can make a good decision for themselves about who to work with. It's not nice to pretend to be something you're not, or to hold back part of yourself in shame. How? First, get the details out for yourself and feel whatever feelings they bring up. Then, meet with a copywriter/editor/messaging type person, who's got an empathetic ear and the savvy to shape that into something clients can relate to. Often, we are not the best person to see how our story might inspire others or make them feel connected to us as humans. Going it alone in this brings up more of the earlier trauma and feeling that you don't have the support you need. So, get help for this step. Seek, and you will find a way to message your difficult truth in ways that are safe and supportive.

QUESTIONS FOR REFLECTION:

- Do you share your values and beliefs in your marketing materials?

- Does your personal truth contain spiritual or religious beliefs? If so, do you share some version of those in your marketing?

- Can you see how difficulties and hardships in your life have shaped who you are?

- Could you be willing to share some of those difficulties and be more transparent about yourself in your business?

Finding your why

More and more in business, people are calling for greater authenticity. The demand for this level of connection wasn't present in business before this time. This brings with it the chance to be more of ourselves at work, to bring our whole selves, which of course, includes our spiritual selves.

To accomplish this, you must be adept at naming your why. Your beliefs about the world and how it can be improved fuel your why. Passion, desire, and deep conviction come from this place. Every small boat sailing on big waters has a keel to keep it upright. Your why acts in the same way. No matter how you are tossed about or acted on by the forces around you, you cannot be knocked over when guided by your deeply held principles.

Your why is how others can tell if they resonate with you and the work you do. As you know, there is no shortage of people who do what you do. If you call yourself an accountant, so do hundreds, if not thousands more. Ditto for therapists, massage therapists, copywriters, and just about every service position you can name. Products are no different. Sure, your widget might be unique in some ways, but chances are, it fills a need in someone's life that could easily be filled by another product. I don't say this to be discouraging in any way. It's simply the truth. There's a silver lining: no one does what you do for the same reason as you, or in the same way as you. Because of this, you can touch a group of people in the world that can hear your message better than anyone else's. They resonate with what you put out, and you resonate with their needs. Articulating your why in your marketing materials creates the bridge between you and them.

The work of Simon Sinek comes to mind with his groundbreaking work on finding your why. His TED talk on finding your why has over 30 million views, and ranks as the third most watched TED talk. Maybe that's due, in part, because our brains are wired for why. Ask any parent who listens to his toddler ask that question a hundred times a day. Our human fascination with story relates to why—stories often come about because of that question and, ironically, answer it, as well.

The mind so fixates on why that sometimes, it can become an obsessive loop. We've all had experiences of using the question of "why" to bemoan negative things that have happened to us. Why did this collaboration go sour? Why did they hire someone other than me? Why does updating my website seem so hard to get right?

Often, one of the first steps in a spiritual or self-growth program stops the focus on why something happened, as this tends to keep us stuck in situations as a victim.

To truly move through something, you must get past your initial urge to look for why it happened, and move into processing the situation and all the learning it has for you. For some, this means honoring the five stages of grief for full expression of their real feelings. For others, it's an active time of seeking spiritual answers or other tools such as therapy or self-inquiry work. You don't want to get stuck in looking for the why when it has to do with blame.

At best, why something happened starts as only a thought or opinion that, when held firmly, becomes a conviction. In other words, whatever story you latch onto for why it happened becomes the basis for your belief. In that capacity, why wields great power. Your convictions and beliefs—positive and negative—become the basis for how your life unfolds. You can limit yourself with these, or empower yourself.

Good news—your mind loves a task. Although potentially negative as a path of seeking why something happened, there's a beneficial way to use this tenacity of the mind: Set it to the task of enacting your why, versus asking why.

Irene runs a well-attended dance studio and produces events for companies. She also runs a bilingual preschool and is a parent herself. She's busy and successful. But when she came to me, she didn't feel her success. She felt like giving it all up. Turns out she was exhausting herself with an internal answer she created to why her childhood had been so difficult. Early in her life, she had decided inside herself that no matter what she did, it wasn't going to make a difference. So even though she was creating success in her life now, she couldn't see it. All her activities were just ways she was trying to finally prove that she could make a difference. In our work together, she had to confront this old story. She realized that it was true that in her childhood she really wasn't able to make much of a difference. She had to grieve how awful that was for her at that time. After releasing a lot of the emotion around the story, she also could see that this was no longer true. It wasn't instant as she had to process a lot and change things in her world that had been built on "proving" instead of her authentic self. This meant leaving her marriage and rearranging her priorities. Today she is living an entirely different life. She's identified her why as making as big of a difference as she can make in the world. Now she can see that she is doing just that in each of her endeavors. Her dance studio is teaching dozens of people confidence through movement. Her events create community and fun for hundreds more. And her preschool is touching the lives of many children and their families. Instead of giving it all up, Irene is living her why by looking at how she can increase the impact of each of these endeavors.

Why don't we all know it—this oh, so important personal why? One reason comes from living in a culture that stresses collective beliefs. Our media doesn't reflect the vast array of human approaches but rather, a select one. The arts aren't celebrated as a part of our cultural expression, but instead as something to be consumed by those who can afford it. Schools aren't set up to elicit the individual thinking of each child. Children are still taught standard truths about grammar, mathematics, and worldview in a school system first developed during the Middle Ages, and systematized during the Renaissance. In other words, we've been teaching the same standardized subject matter to each generation, for four hundred years.

Add to that, the fact that we live in an age in which modern capitalistic approaches to living vastly outweigh indigenous or other approaches. Very few cultures celebrate individuals finding and expressing who they really are, such as coming-of-age rituals. The few who do, mostly celebrate it as a big party like a bar mitzvah or quinceañera, rather than a plan for growth. In modern life, we are not sent on a path of individualism, but rather are asked to buy into a collective approach.

Nevertheless, a spark remains in each of us. Despite the conditioning leading us to draw similar conclusions, many still have a gnawing feeling at some point to bring to light that which they alone feel the call to express in this world.

Becoming aware of this inner impulse and following it can lead you to your why.

Luckily, you may already be enacting some of your why, even if you aren't fully aware of it. Since it lives inside of you, it can push you to make certain decisions, gain specific skills, and start your specific business, even if you can't exactly name it. You may just seem drawn toward certain actions. The universe, in turn, helps you by bringing you experiences and opportunities that resonate with this inner truth. It's common when I help someone find their why that they recognize that it's been at play in their lives all along.

Finding the why of your whole life can take a lifetime. Finding your business why can be simpler. I remember finding my why through a process provided when I was receiving my certification in a Higher Ground Leadership® course. Articulating my why was startling at first, but it did shape the current version of my business. I'm grateful, because it was a pivotal time for me, and I needed some kind of keel to shape my course. Read about my journey with this here: lindabasso. com/find-your-purpose. Realizing my why helped me make decisions throughout that transition. Over time, I've come to see that my why has always been a part of me. I'd just never said it out loud in such a concise way before.

There's no shortage of types of work in the world to help you find your why. Read Simon Sinek's work or follow the same path I did, and use *The Spark, the Flame, and the Torch.* Or here's a simple exercise to get you started.

1. Think of your business and what it does for people, or animals, or the environment. Answer this question: why is it important this gets done? For example, if you style hair, your answer might be that it's important so people look their best. Or, if you repair cars, you might respond that it's important because it gets them where they need to go.

2. Using your answer, ask yourself why that's important. Why is it important for people to look their best or to get where they need to go? You might say that it's important that people look their best so they feel confident about going about their lives. Use this answer and ask yourself why this is important.

3. Keep going by asking, each time, why it's important that your answer happen, always using your last answer as the new subject of "why is it important?" until you've drilled down to some essence that feels meaningful to you.

Here's an example:

I fix cars for people. *Why is that important?* It gets them where they need to go. *Why is that important?* So they can meet their obligations. *Why is that important?* So they can take care of their families. *Why is that important?* Because strong families make life better. *Why is that important?* A better life for each person means a better world. This person's why has to do with making the world a better place.

Another person might answer completely differently, and get to a different why:

I fix cars for people. *Why is that important?* So they can go where they want. *Why is that important?* Getting what you want can make you happy. *Why is that important?* Happy people are nicer to be around. *Why is that important?* Well, maybe we'd have less conflict if people were happy. *Why is that important?* Less conflict might mean more peace. *Why is that important?* To make the world safer. *Why is that important?* Then I wouldn't worry about my grandchildren's future. This person's why has to do with creating happiness for a safer world.

Let whatever comes be good enough. There's no right or wrong. Remember, this starts the exploration into possibility, and this may just be the beginning of your own exploration. In my case, my why boiled down to nurturing others growth, which is truly the keel for everything in my life. But, I hadn't been expressing those things in my business copy. Now I am, and things are much clearer for potential clients.

QUESTIONS FOR REFLECTION:

- Did you get to any essence of your why?

- Do you see examples of this concept in your business or personal life? Give some examples.

- If your why was in the world more, how would the world be better?

- Anything else you can think of that's special about your why?

- Can you imagine sharing your why in your marketing materials?

What you really sell

Purpose-driven entrepreneurs don't go into business only to make money. Even the folks who profess money as their goal are usually trying to create something else for themselves, like freedom or the ability to choose, but that's another story. Purpose-driven entrepreneurs often go into business to make a difference in other people's lives by contributing to their skills and talents, and getting paid for it. They yearn for an alignment of themselves and their work. They want to make the world a better place. That may sound like a greeting card, but times are shifting so that people believe they *can* affect change, even in some small way, to positively affect the world.

Hope starts to replace cynicism. The idealism of the 60s birthed a generation that would grow up loving introspection and self-healing. And, generally, folks who've walked a self-healing path want to give back in some way. Moving to wholeness naturally leads to looking outward to see what you can contribute.

The issue seems to be money. If one could simply contribute to the world and money would somehow appear, there would be a whole lot of happy purpose-driven people out there. In truth, it can be that simple, but in our minds, there's a whole lot of complexity around money. Many of us grew up thinking that money was linked to evil—if not to the devil himself—and to corporations, and all the wrong they do.

In truth, though, money acts as an exchange. Inherently, money connects to neither anything good or bad. The issue comes from us having set up a world where money doesn't just exchange goods, but also connects to the ability to choose, having power over others, and how resources are divided. Money, as a truly neutral exchange, would work only in a society in which basic dignities were respected and the environment was considered sacred.

Inherent in our society are built-in barriers to the access of money. The medium you use to exchange goods cannot also be the measurement used to judge worth, ethics, and justice. In addition, because we also use money to exchange access to life-sustaining food, water, and even access to quality air, money has become entangled with survival. This gives money all kinds of energetic connotations it's not meant to have.

Entrepreneurs face a couple of ways they have to deal with this money issue. First, the notion of selling ourselves, partially because we are the person providing the service, or because the product we sell was created by us. Fascinating, because when you buy a service or product from someone, you don't believe you are buying the other person. You know you are paying them to provide you with a service or product.

But, turn it around, and it feels so personal. As entrepreneurs, we should understand the truth of what we sell is not *us*.

The second issue revolves around the fact that most of us cling to a myriad of limiting beliefs around money. Because we are in business for ourselves, we bring those beliefs into our businesses. If you work for a company, you may have these same limiting beliefs (that affect how much you earn, how much debt you create, and so on), but for the most part, the work comes in, you complete it, and get reimbursed every two weeks with a paycheck. However, when you are in business for yourself and have limiting beliefs around money, you do things like not finding enough clients, making poor business financial choices and often, either not getting your business off the ground or never earning enough from it to be considered a sustainable (let alone a thriving) business. You need to clear out your limiting beliefs so they don't get tangled up with what you sell.

Limiting beliefs around money will show up in how much business you allow yourself to receive.

Think of your truth as an offering you are here to make. Surprisingly, your offering may feel as natural as air to you. So natural you may not often see it within yourself. In your business, it can be a little clearer. It's what you really sell.

Knowing what you *really* sell becomes the cornerstone of marketing in an authentic way. As an entrepreneur, you probably describe your service or product more or less like others in your field—at a surface level. A business coach sells business planning, a bookkeeper sells financial recording, and a music teacher sells music lessons. Why do your clients come to you instead of another company down the street? In reality, your clients are getting something deeper than what you may think you're selling, and you should know that. It becomes the real point of differentiation between you and other businesses providing a similar service or product.

The trick comes to getting down to the essence of what you provide for your clients. It's most powerful when it's one word, but two words or a short phrase will work. The point is to drill down to the essence of what's strongly connected to you and your why.

For example, on the surface, I sell marketing. Like other marketers, I offer knowledge and experience about how to market—what to say and where to say it to get interest in your business. But, there's something deeper. At this deeper level, I sell growth. My clients come to me to grow their businesses via their marketing. When you hire me, it doesn't end there. Over the process of our work, my clients also grow their professional selves, and ultimately, their personal selves. The essence of what I sell is growth, and I provide the nurturing support and strategy to achieve it.

When you know the essence of what you sell, you know how to message your marketing. It makes it easier to market what you do because you have a built-in theme for your messaging—your graphics, your language, indeed, your entire brand. And when your marketing message expresses your essence, it makes it easier for people to recognize whether you are the right fit for them. The bookkeeper who sells balance becomes an ideal match for some, while the one who sells confidence will draw in others. When you communicate your essence, you know how to approach the world in a way that others can truly understand you and what you sell. The payoff? People are much more responsive to your authentic self than they are to the surface you.

And that comes back to your why. Your essence deeply connects to your why. Once you pinpoint what you're selling, step into it. Embrace it. Own it. Lean on it. Use it to guide your marketing for greater results.

If you don't know for sure what you really sell, then find out! Talk to your clients, your family, your friends, and colleagues. They see what you offer more easily than you do. Or, hire someone to help you. Once you have some insights, try on the words or phrases. Dabble, experiment, and be open until the right description settles on you a little more comfortably than the rest. Knowing and articulating your essence makes all the difference. It's the first step to growing yourself and your business. Get ready for transformation!

Here are several approaches to help you understand what you really sell:

1. Think about one or two of your most successful clients. Ones that you feel really got a lot out of working with you and who you enjoyed working with. If you think about where they started before working with you and where they ended up, how would you describe that journey? Free-write on this topic for a few minutes. Afterwards, go back and circle any words or phrases that seem like possible clues to the essence of what you sell.

2. Think of several clients and the actual outcomes they've had with you. List those outcomes. For example, maybe they finished their taxes, straightened out their books, or launched a new service. Maybe they updated their wardrobe, landed a new client, or refreshed their website. In other words, what did working with you give them on a practical level? Now review each client, and muse on whether there was an emotional piece to the job. Did your client get their taxes done and feel relieved? Or, straighten out their books and feel more organized? Do this for each client and look for a strand of commonality among them.

3. If you are having trouble identifying what you sell, try this idea to get your juices flowing. First, decide which

industry you work in. Try to put it into the most generic category. For example, if you are a bookkeeper, then your industry is finance. If you are a realtor, your industry is real estate. If you are a coach, it depends on what type of coaching you do; a health coach is part of the health industry, a leadership coach might be part of the business industry, and a life coach likely would identify with the personal-improvement industry or family services industry. It doesn't matter so much that you choose the right industry, or want to look at multiple industries, as this is just a creative research exercise to find some inspiration. Once you've chosen an industry, then do some general research on this industry. For example, type "finance industry" in a web search and read a couple of the articles that describe this industry. Visit some of the websites that come up. Do you see words or phrases that you identify or resonate with? By depersonalizing your work and looking at the broad strokes of industries you are connected to, you may more easily see the essence of what you do.

4

YOUR REAL OPPORTUNITY

By weaving the practices throughout your day, you have the chance to stay connected with your divinity. To be filled up and replenished as you move along so that you are always full and meeting with others or doing from a full place, not a place of lack. This is the true magic in these practices. From here, all things can be done. – channeled wisdom

Lose the contradiction

If I say "whistle while you work," what pops into your mind (besides the seven dwarfs)? We immediately understand not only what it means, but why it's desirable. Work and leisure or pleasure are related, after all. We generally do one to get the other. Work seems mandatory, i.e., working for the means to get those things that are pleasurable. We now know leisure and pleasure are mandatory for good health and well-being, but it can be difficult to achieve when there are no monetary means. Hence, the intertwined relationship.

Making the best of our work makes sense since this gives us pleasure at work, *and* affords us pleasure after work. Too often, we pit money-making against leisure time. We create a polarization: work vs. fun. Anything that's versus becomes at best, competitive and at worst, antagonistic. That's a difficult vibration to live in, day after day. Competition creates a winner and a loser. Antagonism has two parts: the antagonizer and the agonizer. Who wants either of those as colleagues, day after day, at work?

If you've ever been in therapy, acted in theater improv, or seen a martial art like Aikido or Jujutsu that uses a concept of yielding, you've seen a different way to work with competing energies. Have you ever had a seeming contradiction in your world that worked itself out over time, without either side being right and the other wrong? You hold both concepts as equal without directing a lot of attention to them. You make space for both things to possibly be true. Over time, the tension that existed between the two dissipates. What was seemingly unresolvable becomes integrated as true or acceptable.

For example, let's say you dislike updating your website. You know it needs to be done, but every time you sit down to do it, you feel irritated or distracted. So, you rarely do it, or if you do, there's an afternoon or more of irritation in your world. There are lots of conversations in your head about this whole issue. Why do you do this every time? What's the big deal anyway? Why can't you just do it without all the drama? Or, why do websites have to be updated so often, you fume. Why can't business stuff just be easier? Maybe you share all these thoughts with a friend at happy hour, or complain about it to your spouse after work, or make jokes about how inept you are. All in all, it takes up a lot of space and does not bring any ease into your work life. Another way to do this would be to admit, with no judgment, you have competing, almost opposite desires, in this situation. On one hand, you'd like to have your website updated and at its best. You have a longing for professional, current business materials that make you look good to others. On the other hand, you cannot stand the process that makes it possible. It gets right under your skin and truth be told, you never want to touch your website again. Admitting both these positions might seem hopeless or at least, a little weird. Taught to be rational, most of us are uncomfortable admitting something as irrational as wanting opposite things. If you are honest about your opposing thoughts and can hold both thoughts with no judgment around having them, there will start to be a resolution. At first, it will just be a softening around the whole situation. Neither truth will seem bigger than the other, and you may experience a bit of resignation. At some point, when held long enough, the two will cease to feel like they are in opposition. As crazy as it may seem, you admit that both are really true and that it's ok. There will be little to no emotion left, as you realize you do have to make some choices to either let the website stand unchanged, or put in some time to update it. Drama won't fuel your viewpoint any longer. You'll make decisions that you feel more at peace about and likely, the website will get updated either by you or someone you hire to do it. Truly, magic happens when we make room for both.

Why? It makes room for wholeness in our lives, especially for entrepreneurs who are less effective when in constant tension. Studies show that we humans are uncomfortable when we hold contradictory beliefs.[2] Psychologists call it cognitive dissonance. For example, if you think play is better than work but spend a lot of time working, you are likely to feel uncomfortable during your workday. If you believe pleasure should be enjoyed only after work completes, you may find it difficult to create personal leisure/pleasure time in your personal life, since as an entrepreneur, there is always more work you could do. Or, if you believe sales people are unsavory, you are likely to experience uncomfortable tension between selling (which may feel slimy) and your desire to make your business successful. You may find yourself not only avoiding sales conversations, but also not doing needed marketing activities that might lead to these sales conversations to avoid this tension.

This goes beyond the typical resistance many entrepreneurs have to doing something out of their comfort zone. When faced with cognitive dissonance, we feel so uncomfortable we seek to change beliefs or behaviors to bring ourselves back into congruence. For example, instead of supporting ourselves in growing into a more productive attitude about sales, we may rationalize our not getting to the needed marketing activities with thoughts of being too busy, needing more research, or being unsure what exactly we need to do, which acts to keep us away from the tension. I see many entrepreneurs avoiding some area of their marketing or sales because of these contradictory beliefs.

Combatting the contradictory beliefs doesn't work. The more you deny or ignore the contradiction, the more control it has over your actions. The answer lies in *allowing* the contradiction to come to light and working with it, not against it. Yielding martial arts work because no energy goes to resisting. By allowing the attack, the receiver need only exert a little energy in moving the attack to her advantage. She doesn't block or return the attack initially, but inserts herself into the attack in a way that uses the energy of the attack itself to knock the attacker off balance. In this way, the need for a counter attack can be minimal or goes away entirely. *Flowing with* creates less resistance and in turn, needs less energy on your part to respond. Therapy and coaching both have many tools to create this state, too.

Use yes instead

Another approach to working around resistance comes from the "Yes, and ..." approach, so popular in theater improv trainings.

Today, it's increasingly common to see improv training used in corporate or leadership settings to help executives become better decision makers. Improv classes have been taught at Duke, Columbia, UCLA, Harvard and MIT Sloan, and used by companies such as American Express, DuPont, Ford, PepsiCo, Procter & Gamble, Twitter, Google, and Fidelity. People who take improv classes improve their ability to listen, go with the flow, and manage the unexpected. They tap into their creativity and are better at teamwork. Saying "no" stops the action and so does "Yes, but…" With improv training, the negative goes away. You learn the positives of failure and how to cope when something doesn't work.

The improv based "Yes, and…" approach simply means that no matter what happens around you, your response must always be "yes, and," at which point you add new ideas and comments. You aren't allowed to say "no" or "yes, but …" This works in comedy improv with hilarious results.

This technique creates acceptance. It shows you how to not push against what is. When you can live life in terms of seeing what's happening and only adding to it, you are both stepping into flow and accepting that while reality may not be what you want it to be, you can only build on the reality of the present. Using this accepting approach can restore harmony to our day-to-day life. It lets us be our whole selves, interacting with others in positive, life-affirming ways.

This doesn't just affect us. We are each involved with circles of people—our families, friends, co-workers, and communities—that are all affected by our participation with them. If everyone runs around with this energy of contradiction, it creates a group, nation, possibly a globe, of people who are in resistance to their own lives. The skills used in improv can help you feel safe in a group because you learn that no matter what, you're all working together. "Yes, and" can increase your ability to make a contribution as you learn to toss in your ideas. You realize trust comes from building upon each other's ideas rather than negating one another, and striving to have your ideas be right.

Don't aim to just feel better during your workdays. To think of work only as obligation or monetary reward misses the point. Work could be part of the means *and meaning* for our lives. We all long to contribute to ourselves and our community. Your work steps in as a primary way to do that. Winning looks like being happy and grateful for the work you do each day, and feeling as though your work makes up a blissful part of why you are on this planet.

Your livelihood should support, not punish you.

When enough of us as individuals win, all of humanity begins to win. We are empathic beings, who are collective by nature. We are biologically, emotionally, and spiritually primed to take in the attitude or vibration of the people around us. If you're a parent, you see this in action when you realize parenting happens by modeling, not talking. If you are surrounded by people with attitudes of defeat and despair, you have a high chance of feeling similar. Ditto if the people around you are happy and in their bliss because of the contribution they are making. In other words, as we begin to lift people up, it creates a ripple effect, and many people are lifted up.

Speaking of uplifted—happier people are healthier, experience less stress, and live longer. Don't believe me? Google it for yourself. I found 14 studies that said just that. Happiness lowers heart disease, strengthens your immune system, and feels less painful, in lives that last longer than unhappy people[3].

As I sit here writing today, I found 101 pages of books when I typed in "happiness" on Amazon. At 12 to 16 books per page, that's a lot of information on how to be happy! This goes beyond health and wellness. Happier people develop more resiliencies to cope with what's not working, transform their lives for the better, and head towards a flourishing life[4].

What does this mean for the collective planet? Happy people tend to give more to charity, do more volunteer work, and participate in their community. They are less cautious dealing with others, believing most people are fair and helpful[5]. They are more productive at work, more creative at solving problems, and better at negotiating[6].

People who experience negative emotions, on the other hand, tend to act in opposite ways. They get stuck and live in states of stress which encourage them to attack or flee[7].

Here's what my guides say about it:

If you shift the frequency of activities on your planet, you will be able to shift the frequency of the planet. Instead of violence happening frequently, peace can flourish. Instead of depression spreading, happiness can. Instead of abuse, safety. And, on and on. The importance of up leveling your frequency cannot be understated. You have a collective history of focusing on what doesn't work. You must shift this to see what does work, so you can increase it. By spending your days immersed in practices that lift your heart, feed connection, and bring ease, you will change the collective experience.

It's true that each of you have a personal opportunity as well as the collective one just discussed. This can be something you are called to do to enhance other's lives or the environment around you. It encompasses every possible contribution you can make, big and small. Your job comes in finding yours and to the best of your ability moving it forward.

QUESTIONS FOR REFLECTION:

- Can you name any contradictions you hold related to marketing?

- Is it possible to hold both of these contradicting points as true for you?

- Can you imagine getting to "yes, and…" about these contradictions?

How family ties can bind

One of the most effective ways to find your contribution and move forward is to break family patterns. If you look back through the generations of your family, you will see a long line of behaviors such as: money mishandling, dysfunctional communication, illness, anger management issues, depression, passive aggressive or control issues, workaholism, neglect, intimacy issues, playing below one's potential, lack of boundaries, alcohol or drug use, unplanned children, abuse, crime and so on, persisting across the generations. If you can step back far enough with an objective eye, you can name the patterns existing in your family. These are the issues the group you've come to be part of has chosen to explore, work with, and know intimately.

Enrique grew up in a family that has a wide range of behaviors around clarity in pursuing one's own path. Because they are from Central America, which has a reputation for being both laid back and overly enmeshed with family influence, it's easy to say it's a cultural thing. However, friends of Enrique's family don't display this same range of patterns around self-determination. Among the siblings of each generation, there seem to be three personality types: the pursuer, who determines what he wants and does it; the actor, who doesn't pursue her own dream but supports others dreams by her actions; and the victim, who believes their own circumstances are too difficult to accomplish much of anything. They act this pattern out over and over, every generation. It's not even one side of the family—the marriages that take place within the family bring in other families, who also have this pattern. This, of course, impacts their work lives, as some members of the family pursue their work dreams as entrepreneurs, while others are busy working to make other's dreams come to fruition, and still, others aren't working at all. This pattern shows up in their monetary lives also, as some in the family build wealth, others maintain it, and others spend it. The first two times Enrique tried to become an entrepreneur, the pressures of this pattern were too difficult to overcome. He struggled to believe that he could not only decide his own future, but also bring it into being. He eventually went to work for a corporation that allowed him a fair amount of autonomy. He's splitting the supporter role vs. the dream-builder role in this job, as some things are under his direction and some things are supporting others. For now, he chooses this compromise—some structure and stability mixed with some self-determination—while he works to overcome this family pattern. His hope is to let enough of the pattern go that he can someday step into his own business in a healthy way.

Every generation makes strides to overcome these patterns. Some make large steps, others tiny. It's the attempt that matters. When you feel as though you are going it alone, remember you are part of a collective, and every member in your group does their part to move it along. Even the ones who are doing something bad are part of the process, as these folks may have agreed to be instigators within the group, so that others could do their growth work. You may not always like it, but you can celebrate that you are part of a bigger whole, where everyone is sharing in it together.

If you keep reacting within this whole, it will keep moving forward. Sometimes it looks like stepping away when it's expected you'll stay, so another may feel the loss and be moved to reflect on how it happened, rather than sitting back and blaming. Or, if they choose to blame, you get to demonstrate that hurtful behaviors will no longer be tolerated. In other words, if you are continuing to assess, digest, and act on what's happening within the group, you are doing your part.

Why does this matter to your marketing? Family patterns don't just apply to your personal life. The beliefs the generations of your family hold about money, working, independence, trust, communication, and self-worth directly contribute to your ability to be successful in running your own business. I saw this so often in my clients that I became a coach, rather than consultant, so I had the training and tools to help them through these issues. I tell all my clients that if you're going to grow your business, you have to grow yourself. Why? Because, you aren't the person you need to be to run that larger business. I explain to them: Here you are, the size you are, and the size your business is. Over here, is where you want your business to grow. But, you aren't that person yet! So, you have to become that person—the one capable of running, managing, selling, and fulfilling in that new, larger business. Doing that often means growing beyond the limiting, defeating, critical stances you may have inherited from your families.

How do you know if you have a family pattern to overcome in your marketing?

- **Direct:** Parents or family members who fear you won't make it if you own your business rather than work for a company. Raised in a generation that valued the safety or financial security companies seemed to promise, this family member worries you're taking the wrong course. This comes up around your marketing, as that's the most visible place in your business. Some ways this plays out: family members see your email about your next course or upcoming talk, and call you to see if you're sure about this business. Or, they sigh and look distressed when you speak about your work, tell you about jobs they've heard of, or send contacts to you of people they believe could give you a company job, even in a different industry.

- **Indirect:** Family members may not talk about your business at all, though this smacks of the same fears as the direct approach. They ask how you are, how the kids are, about your health, and tell you all their updates without once ever mentioning your work life. When you bring it up, it's met with vague responses, like "that's good" or "oh, interesting" with no follow-up conversation. You are left feeling like the invisible person in a room full of others.

- **Joking:** Your comments or discussions about your work are met with light teasing or meant-to-be funny comments. This might sound as though the person is interested or supportive, but if you look back on the conversation, there was no substance exchanged. Even when it seems like they are asking in earnest, they ask with a joking comment that, if you listen to the actual words, could be interpreted as critical. Something like, "Hey, how's life for my favorite self-employed slacker?" Or, when you are explaining something about the business, you may hear, "Oh, must be really hard working whenever you want to," or some other joking comment instead of responding to what you are saying. This approach may seem harmless, but also indicates a fair level of uncomfortableness, either in a fear for you or a comparison for them, as they fight back their own desires for more autonomy or living their dream.

- **Self-sabotage:** When you are thinking about a new service, preparing for a presentation to get new business, or doing some other marketing effort, you have an internal reaction that seems like one of the above. You either directly question your abilities or your reasons for being in business. You may express doubt about the sanity or safety of this effort. You may find yourself asking if it's time to get a real job. Or, you disconnect from yourself and feel numb, unable to access your ideas and creativity, unable to bring yourself to focus on the marketing piece. Or, you push on, making jokes to yourself and others, about what you're up to.

- **Marking time:** You keep taking steps in your marketing but nothing seems to work out. Every time you start to gain momentum, you find yourself pulling back or getting overly stressed. It seems as though you should be making more progress, but somehow you aren't. Or you've been having successes, but at some point, they stop cold, and you are left at the same level of success you've had for a while.

- **Overwork:** You are making progress in your marketing efforts, but they take a lot of work. Each effort brings more business but also more work, and you wonder if you can keep going. You are busy but not taking steps to do things differently, like setting up systems, so you can be more graceful with your time and efforts. You might consider growing your business but dismiss it because that would require so much more work and that marketing effort. You are not energized by your efforts, but rather, feel drained.

If you identify with something in the above list, it's likely you have some inherited family beliefs about money, success, or safety holding you back. You'll need to address these head on and recover from them to grow. Even the first three, which are enacted by other people toward you, rather than something you are bringing up, mean you have some work to do. It's impossible to have a family member acting in these ways toward you without creating an internal response on your part, even if you are unaware of it.

These steps can help you begin to untie the family cords holding you back:

1. Identify the way it's showing up from the list above. Ask yourself what family patterns are playing out to cause this reaction, either from the other person or inside yourself. If you don't resonate with what's listed above, but think you may have family issues at play, start paying attention to what family ties may be impacting your business today.

2. Let the universe answer your question about what family patterns are at play. Live with the question over the next few days. You may find yourself recalling phrases from your family, life, or situations around money or work that were playing out as you grew up. You might have a dream connected to this question. You might read an article or find a book that brings something to mind. Trust what comes to you if it seems to answer this question.

3. Take time to journal or discuss this idea with someone you trust. Often, I muse to my spouse during a questioning time like this, and he often sees something I don't. Or, while writing in a journal without censoring yourself, you may suddenly start remembering important issues.

4. When you see what some of the inherited patterns are, decide to deal with them directly. If the patterns are about money, consider educating yourself about finance so you have a more realistic view of it, or work with a financial counselor to make plans and budgets for your goals. If the patterns are about success, consider therapies and healing modalities that deal with self-worth. If you have family patterns that are related to safety, then you

may need to heal from trauma or abuse that happened earlier in your life, or in your parent's lives.

Take regular action on healing these patterns. They do not go away if left unattended, and in my experience, wreak havoc on entrepreneurs' business lives. Why not devote some of your non-working hours to bolstering yourself so you can show up clean and clear in your business?

Identify your purpose

Most entrepreneurs have the following goal: breaking free within their professional life to do what fulfills them, while using their gifts and talents to contribute. For some, this means letting go of grandiose ideas of contribution, and focusing on where they can make a difference with what's in front of them. For others, this means stepping out of a deadening, safe or comfortable situation to contribute their real gifts and talents. In either case, doing so will feel profoundly uncomfortable for most. Why? Because, they are being asked to grow into a state different from where they currently are.

As you explore your real purpose, consider nature. When you spend time in nature, you begin to see the multitudes of patterns, and tiny details, that are part of every living thing. Attention to detail and design radiates from even in the most minute bud. Study nature a bit, and you'll see an intelligent eco system. Every piece of our planet seems designed for a purpose. My guides define these purposes as either holding, growing, being, receiving, or pushing. Turns out, purpose can be an energetic thing, not just a doing thing.

Does one of these energies resonate with you? Try to identify the energies you belong to, and which you offer to others. Viola, you see a part of your purpose. As I've discussed, mine is around growth. My husband's is holding. The one you belong to causes some struggle, as you are here to learn how to be in this energy. You will seek others who do it well, so you can learn to do it better. Others will seek you for what you do well, so they can learn to do it, too. Hence, driven people may find themselves surrounded by people who are laid back and simply receive in life. The driven person is trying to learn to just be. On the other hand, the laid-back person wants to learn to push. There is a purpose in both, and purpose in coming together.

Beyond purpose, the real opportunity for your business sits at the edge of your consciousness, beckoning to you. Think of that activity or impact within reach for your business that is bigger than you can imagine, farther away than you can see, and yet, it still calls to you. For most, it's a bit scary to contemplate, though, with all its energy, it can feel extremely exciting, as well.

I can think of dozens of clients who've come to me with the idea that there is something bigger calling them from within their business. Usually it's that they've been doing their work for awhile and are starting to see the impact their work is really making. Perhaps they thought they were teaching clients conscious movement, but were really helping them drop old limitations and accept themselves. Or that they were offering them image and beauty consulting but their clients were actually learning to stand up for themselves. Possibly their business started because they took a certain kind of training, and at first, only worked with their clients in that way but over time developed their own version of the work. Then the urge to share it in a bigger way, or make a larger contribution starts calling. The idea to speak on a larger stage, touch more lives, or create their own brand comes up in visualizations with their businesses. Usually they feel disbelief, like "who me?!?" when they see this possible future. Excitement comes, too, as they contemplate how their life could change and how their work could grow. Only about a third begin to step forward toward this new reality, as the rest tuck it away as not the right time or realize that growing is not something they are up for. Those who step forward begin a journey that stretches them in ways they couldn't have guessed at. Sometimes they arrive where they meant to go, other times their path veers along the way and they go somewhere else. But all look back on the ride as a journey where they grow into a bigger, better version of themselves.

The real opportunity for all of us is the elevation of our planet. To lift the vibrational frequency to a point where we transcend much of the lower or heavy vibrational experiences we currently experience. Leaving behind low vibration energies like guilt, shame, and doubt to live in the lighter states of acceptance, joy and love. This process has been happening for years, but recently there has been a shift in the energies making it possible to speed things along exponentially. Have you noticed the change? It's sort of like shoveling snow or a digging dirt. At first, it seems like each shovel full only moves a little bit. Over time, since a lot has been cleared, each scoop seems to move a lot. Soon, with only little bits left, it's easy to push it away with your boot—or even to finally clear it with one good breath.

QUESTIONS FOR REFLECTION:

- Do you identify with one of these purpose energies: holding, growing, being, receiving, or pushing?

- Do you see how others in your life hold other energies of purpose you may need to learn?

- Does this help you see opportunities for you to contribute to others or the environment?

- Does an opportunity call in your work that scares or excites you?

5

IT REALLY MATTERS

"Focusing on matter is one of the only things that matters where you are. This wordplay is well intended. Matter is the main way that you navigate and effect your lives, yet you often act like it's just stuff around you." – channeled wisdom

Affecting matter moves you forward

Our culture's story of success centers around it being hard to obtain. The higher up you go, the harder it becomes. I want you to know that it doesn't have to be that way. This myth helps us stay comfortably seated where we are, rather than pursuing the changes that even though they might make us happy, might also feel very uncomfortable while we are making them. Think about every fairy tale or hero's journey you've ever read. Although they enjoy a happy ending, would any of the main characters have agreed to their journey beforehand? No way.

Instead, focus on *affecting matter* rather than making change. What does this mean? Let's start by defining matter—you know, the stuff they defined in 8th grade science class as the physical things all around us.

Matter differs from energy. This is a good distinction for purpose-driven folks who tend to focus on energy more than physical matter. Sure, as spiritual beings, we tend to focus on the energetic. As Pierre Teilhard de Chardin said, we are spiritual beings having a physical existence—with emphasis on the physical as the full other half of being spiritual. In this arena which we all call life, it turns out we interact most with our creator in the physical plane.

In other words, it's not enough to only tend to the spiritual side of our nature. We were designed to be here, now, in the physical with all that entails. Forget outdated notions of transcending our lowly human desires in search of something more divine. When we honor our physical bodies as temples—that our spirit resides in—we are creating a profound partnership. When we honor the needs and desires of our bodies as a way of being in conversation with the divine, life here on earth mimics heaven above.

Say my guides:

> If life is a cosmic dance between you and your maker, the environment or physical world around you is the stage where it all takes place. So, pay close attention to the experiences around you, as they are your dance with the divine. In other words, acting and receiving feedback is exactly what you are here to do. This is your spiritual practice in many senses. Your job is to shift your internal state to one that focuses on affecting response in your external environment.

Turns out we are very powerful in enacting matter. Trouble is, we don't often spend time in deliberately affecting things because we spend too much time worrying about what's the matter. A little humor with my words, but don't overlook my point. You are here to enact a difference with matter. Yet, so many of us are afraid to act. Or, don't use the info coming back to us to change how we engage with matter.

For example, take a person or situation you are having difficulty with. Instead of playing with the situation as if you were a creator and could affect an outcome, you push the situation away. You tell yourself you don't have time or that you shouldn't have to deal with this person or situation. We are still in a plane where every action has an opposite reaction; so as you push them away, they come forward more strongly. If, instead, you bend toward them, they will bend away from you. This matters to the entrepreneur because often we have difficulty with our vendors, assistants, or other support people. Or we are distracted at work by a personal interaction that is difficult.

Just how do you bend toward a person or situation that you are upset by? Start by first, accepting that you want to deal with the situation, not run from it. Just giving yourself the permission to step toward it brings in your power. Then use the tools you have available to you, like changing your interior state, prayer, intention, or energetic clearing. Don't keep engaging with it on a superficial physical level where you make it about right and wrong. Clear out your personal feelings and what gets stirred up by the person or situation, and you will find it starts to untangle and bother you less. Use all your senses to engage in matter, and be impressed with what you can create.

How does this affect marketing? Exactly the same—you need to focus on affecting matter. In coaching, we have the philosophy of playing for results. If the focus centers on what you can create rather than only outcomes, then you have a better chance of moving matter.

Nina was just starting a new marketing campaign when she and I met. Recognizing I might have a piece she was missing, I suggested we have a phone conversation to discuss where she was in the beginning of her new effort. In a few short minutes, I sensed she was feeling overwhelmed, alone, and completely exhausted by all that needed to be done to have a successful outcome for her campaign. Her problem wasn't that she couldn't see what needed to be done; it was that she was approaching all that needed to be done as an obligation that carried great consequences if things didn't go well. In addition, a lot of what needed to be done was not in her skill set, or were tasks she really didn't like doing. No wonder she was exhausted!

She hired me during that call, not so much because I had the correct credentials in marketing, but because I pointed out a way for her to get more support in doing the things that weren't her sweet spot. I helped her see that if she fully showed up and played with getting results on many small tasks, she could, indeed, meet the goals of her campaign. She cried with relief during our conversation that someone could see her tired, parched soul struggling to do something important in her business, but going about it in a way that would only bring her the very thing she feared—failure. Instead of taking on the whole project and slugging through it with drudgery, she started looking at what result she could create with the next task. Within five days, she found some friends and colleagues who were willing to brainstorm with her, keep her accountable, remind her to have fun, and to do her activities from love. She creatively found a way to fund an assistant to help her with the administrative parts of the project that made Nina want to hide under her bed. Now, she could turn her attention to where she had the most power: making connections with the people who could fund her campaign.

Not that stepping into this part of the campaign was easy for Nina. She had to work through issues around not bothering others, and ideas around needing the support of others; meaning, she wasn't doing something right, but now, she could focus on affecting changes in this one part of the campaign, instead of being overwhelmed with the whole. She began to experiment or play with affecting the outcome of just the next call or the next few hours, which freed her up to be herself and start enjoying the moments. The results speak for themselves: not only was her campaign a success (she earned more than she had planned), she had new-found confidence in connecting with others, and was offered a record deal for the album she was funding.

Do these results sound miraculous? You bet. In truth, all of us have the potential of meeting or exceeding our goals, but most of us stop ourselves when feeling overwhelmed and not getting the support we need. Rather than break our focus down to the next small action we can take, or look at our business and efforts with playfulness and ease, we focus on all that's not going well. No small business or small business persons can survive the amount of negativity that comes when they focus on what's not working or what could go wrong. Instead, a more positive approach is needed.

In coaching, we use a tool called *playing for results* that looks at breaking down a project into goals and outcomes, and experimenting to see how you might meet those goals. Your focus shifts to not whether you meet those goals, but how the actions you're taking are bringing results that either propel you toward the goal, or push you away from it. If you can bring in the discipline of not getting caught in the story of what it will mean to meet or not meet your goal, you can be more present in the actions you're taking. Being neutral about whether the actions are taking you toward or away from the goal gives you more power to take different actions and change directions more easily. This is in line with the objective focus I spoke of around moving matter. You aren't as concerned with where the matter ends up as you are with how you are influencing it.

Here's an exercise on playing with matter in marketing to get results:

Pick one small marketing goal in your business, one you're not sure how to reach. Brainstorm—by yourself or with your coach or a colleague—many ideas that might move you toward that goal. Go for 10 ideas at least! Twenty would be even better. Choose several of these ideas and experiment with enacting each idea over the coming week. Treat it like a game you are playing. Track whether the actions you take on each idea move you toward your goal or not. Remember, don't judge whether the movement is good or not! You want to keep as neutral a response as you can.

- If the actions are not moving you toward your goal, how can they be changed to get a different result?

- If they are moving you toward your goal, do you need to keep doing them or could it be time for another action to come in?

- If you can't answer these questions, have a colleague or coach listen to you talk them out. Chances are you do have the answers, you just might not be hearing them from yourself.

This continual focus on taking actions in your business to see if they move you forward or backward instead of whether they get the end result, can be a great discipline for a successful business. It can strip away some of the anxiety, and free up space for more enjoyment and creativity. Try it and see for yourself. If you'd like, download a worksheet here lindabasso.com/reluctantmarketer.

There's nothing wrong with you

I often hear clients asking, "What's wrong with me?" Please know this: there may be matter to move or affect, but there is never anything intrinsically wrong with you. This question comes as an unfortunate side effect of living in a culture that doesn't affirm our divinity and perfection. There are a few reasons for this:

1. Our culture tends to focus on the things outside of ourselves we achieve, rather than enjoying the process of getting there. Instead of growing up learning about how to enjoy affecting matter around you, you probably grew up wondering how to get to where you wanted to go and possibly feeling uncomfortable about where you were in the process.

2. Even those with healthy childhoods reach a time in their adolescence when they realize they are alienated from the people around them. This is a natural, biological part of becoming an independent adult. Traditional cultures handled this natural occurrence with rites of passage to help teens through this transition, but our modern life has stripped this away. If teens don't come through this period with a reconnection to their spiritual life, evidence shows this creates a deep emptiness that drives them to fill the void with substances and behaviors that don't really get at the itch. They're left with the feeling that something feels amiss.

3. A third reason comes along because many of us had some kind of dysfunction happening as we grew up. Maybe there was substance abuse—ranging from

social drinking to alcoholism—or emotionally distant families or members, or those who were unskilled in communication. Perhaps your parents were highly judgmental, overly righteous, or too strict. Possibly, you saw the adults around you model being passive victims instead of powerful parents. Or, you simply had caregivers that focused on your physical existence without a thought to your spiritual side. Whatever your flavor of childhood angst, life didn't feel right. As a result, that question—What am I doing wrong?—kept surfacing. You concluded that you must have something wrong with you, you're not good enough, not lovable, not wanted, and on and on. We humans all take things very personally when God really doesn't. It's all energy, and the good and bad are both equally valid experiences. Remember, God shows in all. It's a paradox: everything is deeply personal and not at all personal.

Bringing this all back to marketing, play with matter to see what results you get. Matter can be other people. Make a connection and see where it goes. Your collateral counts as matter. Make some and see what response you get. The web makes a perfect place for it; make something online, and push it out to see where it goes and what comes back. The underpinnings are loose and energetic. If you can step into playing with these bits of matter to see what occurs, you can create a sense of flow, and all those pesky to dos on your marketing list can feel easier and more organic, rather than a long, never ending list. You can't have your marketing wrapped up in what you are worth, or being accepted or rejected. That's not what it's about. It's about playing with matter and seeing what happens.

Something curious happens when you focus on affecting matter. It's almost never a straight line between you and what outcome you are trying to affect. Things often meander when you are moving toward what you want. You see a goal, start playing with matter to achieve it, and then, either life intervenes or you get distracted or become fearful. Things go to the left, then right, then later, you may find yourself back on or near your original path, wondering what in the heck happened!

Why? Because, although you think in a linear fashion, the cosmos does not move that way. Instead, it moves in more of a circular, spiral effect and to be honest, with plenty of chaos. Which can be terrifying to you now, but as you increase your consciousness, you'll find it not so difficult to thrive within. This all begins to make total and complete sense—just not in the way you currently see time and space.

There are many realities and sets of time happening at the same time. As a result, it often takes more than a straight line to connect two or more things. So, some weaving of experience and people sometimes has to happen first in order to bring about the correct or highest outcome. Similarly, this concept can also make some things happen instantaneously: you think you'd like to do something, and voila, the very person or thing you need arrives on your doorstep. That's because when things are aligned, energy can be moved from one set of time through the layers into another by reaching through.

Here are some principles that can help us navigate the circuitous nature of the cosmos.

1. *You can never be in the wrong place.* Many of you are in jobs or life experiences you want to change, yet you don't want to change your state of mind or integrate the situation in a way that satisfies the learning you originally wanted from the situation. As a result, you stay or repeat the experience until you do. If you grasp that you are never, ever in the wrong place, you can stop obsessing about why you got there, or why you can't leave and get to the business at hand. Which means

to make the best of the situation for now so you can learn what you need to from the situation.

2. This may create resistance in many of you, but there's only one other choice: *continue to rail against the present and be unhappy.* Instead, make the best of the situation and at least, experience some measure of peace. By shifting your attention toward how to make things even slightly better, you are starting from what *is*. This puts you in the only power position in the universe. Tremendous capacity exists in the present moment, which explains why presence and mindfulness are being talked about so much these days.

3. *In this powerful spot, you begin creating something new.* It may feel only slightly new, which can feel disappointing, but I promise if you begin to master this at the level where you are right now, you will move forward. Someday, you won't have to make these slight adjustments— but for now, remember you are an apprentice. Start shifting things: external situations, internal beliefs and thoughts, until the situation becomes easier to tolerate. This creates the only way out: *through* the situation. As mentioned above, you are never in the wrong place because a) you can head in any other direction as soon as you'd like and b) the training you are receiving, by being in a difficult situation and learning to shift it, puts you on the path of becoming a powerful creator.

4. *Once you are a powerful creator, you are almost never in situations you consider wrong because you simply shift things as needed.* This doesn't mean bad things don't happen, or you're never faced with situations requiring courage, or you don't feel sorrow. Powerful creators often deal with all those things in the same day! They are proficient at processing big emotions and enjoy the surfing of life because they have the skill and courage to do so.

5. *Sometimes the things you dream about or want to happen take some weaving.* You are asking from one vantage point, so you often can't see what's in the way of it coming to fruition. This requires trust. That doesn't mean you can't work toward your dream, but things will never fall into place from your efforts alone. You can only surf waves you are close to. Trust that the weaving will happen toward creating the highest and best outcome.

The reason weaving and joining sometimes takes time can come from many of your dreams involving other people or situations that have not yet come to be. Which means there are a complicated number of variables that must shift in order to bring the situation into being.

The best way we can deal with this circuitous nature of the cosmos is to affect what you can, and trust in what you can't. I'm reminded of the Serenity Prayer, which started off as a sermon by Reinhold Niebuhr and later was popularized by 12-step programs:

God grant me the serenity
to accept the things I cannot change;
courage to change the things I can;
and wisdom to know the difference.

When I first heard it, I was immediately caught by the wisdom in the words. How profound and simple. What I didn't know was the second verse:

Living one day at a time;
enjoying one moment at a time;
accepting hardships as the pathway to peace;
taking, as He did, this sinful world
as it is, not as I would have it;

trusting that He will make all things right
if I surrender to His Will;
that I may be reasonably happy in this life
and supremely happy with Him
forever in the next.
Amen.

Now, even if you don't have a belief in a Christian male god or ideas of sin and an afterlife, you likely can see the wisdom in taking things one day at a time, and not trying to push against what we aren't in direct control of. Sure, life can be hard for each of us, and when it feels that way there can be a lot of pain and suffering. The sun always shines again, and most of us are left more at peace when we work through a painful patch in our lives. By accepting that things are working out in the right way, even though we may not yet see how, we are in a stance of trust. From that place, we can savor much peace and harmony.

Understand how valuable you are

Another aspect of self-worth involves being in the right place at the right time. You have tremendous worth in part because of coming here at a certain time, to a certain place, within a certain group of other beings. In other words, your worth is in what you came here to experience and contribute. – channeled wisdom

I see the marketplace changing. Rather than buying from faceless companies, many of us will choose to work with and purchase only from those we find appealing in some way, or somehow, believe in and trust to solve our issues. Rather than just buying something, we want to come together with others whose products or services can add to what we're doing. I believe that we'll no longer make our decisions based solely on logical sense but rather a feeling of resonance.

So, as a business owner it's important that you, too, show up in a way your clients can resonate with. For successful marketing, you need to be your best brand ambassador and to do this you must believe in your own worth. Thinking you are not worthy may be the bane of human existence—believing the things outside yourself define who you are, or that feedback from others can impact who you are. The bible teaches us it's impossible that anything from the outside can defile you; rather, your inner thoughts are too often impure or wrong. Other spiritualties teach this in a different way. But, all point to believing in our worth. So, work to constantly purify what you believe on the inside. This creates self-worth from the inside out.

Say my guides:

You keep coming to your planet at specific times. If you don't believe in reincarnation, you can think about this in terms of living at one specific time. Why did you come to this planet at this certain time? Why now? Because you have a certain set of qualities, skills, and attributes that make you a good fit for the time you came to live in. This includes your work, of course. Which means you have the exact set of qualities, skills, and attributes making you the perfect fit for your business, and the contributions it can make to the world at this moment. You were given a toolbox of qualities to come here and complete a mission.

Doing your marketing in a way that your business thrives signals your acceptance of that mission.

You came to a specific geographical location on the planet, which also creates value. Again, you brought certain skills and attributes well suited to influence this geo region in your life and business. Temperament, natural inclination, and the ability to adapt are all factors in the relationship between you and your geographical location which work either in harmony or in contrast to create a series of results throughout your business life. This remains true even when you move. It's why you are drawn to go to or stay in certain places during your life. These results move along not only the human experience, but the universal one. How valuable is that? Your participation in your business moves along, not only your own life, but the universal human experience. If you really take in this idea, you can feel valuable in everything you do—even your marketing—no matter how mundane or small it seems.

Who you came here to be with matters, too. You choose people both to grow with through harmony, and through conflict. You also choose people who can protect and nurture you, as well as choose those who can hurt and push you. Again, your participation with the people around you matters so much to the universe. You could be an influence on another that shifts their life and they on you. Would you feel more valuable if you accepted this sacred contract with others to shape the world? Couldn't your marketing be a way of accepting this relationship with others? Marketing makes you visible to them, and helps them become your client so you can make this exchange.

This keeps humanity evolving. It's not random that each generation attempts to do things in an upgraded way. Solving disease, slavery, child labor—even moving from cave to middle ages to modern times—came not as a product of technology, but rather, human innovation and growth of consciousness. It happens from the confluence of these factors. Beings continuing to come here works because they come with just the right mixture of these three things to do their work: where, who, and when. It's no accident where you are, who you're with, and when you've come. If you can sit in that, you might soak in how valuable you are in the scheme of things. This can change everything about your marketing—you can come from a place of confidence, secure in the knowledge you are needed at this time on this planet.

Perhaps, on a soul level, you came to promote independence and growth. Then, from an energetic standpoint, you may have chosen a country or region to grow up in where this either gets frowned upon, or happens but in ways that are not healthy. Why? Because, if you were born in an area where people were healthily independent and growing, what would you learn about these things? Nothing, because they would just be normal to you. You wouldn't add anything to the human collective unless you digest these ideas in some way and bring out your original stamp on them. So, maybe you were born into a family so wealthy you never learned to do things on your own. Or, you were born somewhere that were expected to be compliant and follow the pack. Because of this, you may have negative experiences as you try to promote the need for independence and growth, or enact your soul's mission. Eventually, through the struggle, you find your way with these things. Maybe you grew up with no idea of independence and have a hard time as a young adult when suddenly you have to make your own way in your business and promote yourself. You mess up, learn lessons, and eventually figure out your version of being independent. Along the way, you influence the people around you either by pushing back against their behavior or allowing them to shape yours. In this, you are adding to the collective pool around independence and growth. Or, perhaps, you grew up where you were expected to be compliant, and ended up going your own way, leaving the group behind. Your loss shapes the group you left and you end up learning all the lessons of being alone and rebuilding community. You end up running your business in a way that creates community, or teaching clients how to create community, or just being a thriving business that contributes to your community. Whatever you end up enacting, you are shaping what we humans know about growth and independence through your life and business. This makes you extremely valuable.

Even though you are valuable for what you came to do and who you came to do it with, there's more. Let's remember we are spiritual beings, and our worth cannot be measured. There is nothing you need earn or do for that to be so. Every religion and spirituality I've ever come across says the same. This becomes crucial to embrace as an entrepreneur, since low worth can be one of the biggest reasons your business may fail. So, how can we step more fully into our own worth and be the magnificent divine entrepreneurs we are?

1. *"I AM" meditation:* In yoga, we do a lot of focused breathing to activate our inner state of divinity. If you breathe in/out for a few minutes with a focused attention on the words "I AM" you are invoking an ancient original proclamation of your connection to the universal reality of all that is. Some use the Sanskrit version of the words "So 'ham" (pronounced "SO hum") instead of the English words. The burning bush told Moses these words when he asked God's name, and the Vedics have used the Sanskrit mantra for hundreds of years. We don't have to know why it works to use it. It's powerful and takes only a few minutes whenever you remember to do it. I think it's a way we let our unconscious minds realize we are connected directly to the divine. Do this anytime you need a divine pick me up in your marketing. Perhaps before giving that speech, or presentation, or servicing your clients.

2. *Trust where you are.* Yes, there are things you want that haven't come to fruition yet. Yes, you make mistakes. Yes, your to-do list never stops. Yes, perhaps you need to change directions in your work, upgrade your materials or relationships with vendors. And, yes, all this can be true because life meanders through process before it ends. Along the way, it's all good. So are you. If you can

develop trust in yourself and your path, a whole lot of drama will drift away. You'll be left with space for your divinity to arise. As many mindfulness paths put forth, when you stop agitating the water on the surface, the depths of your peace can become known. This doesn't mean accepting things you'd like to change; it means not torturing yourself with blame and shame while you make needed changes and move forward in life with a peaceful heart. For some, the reminder of this will be enough. For others, you'll need to explore behavioral therapies, meditation, or other kinds of healing to get to this place of trust. It's worth the effort as the more present you are in your marketing, the more effective it tends to be.

3. *Take accurate stock and stop being stingy with yourself.* Sit down and write out all the things you are good at. I mean everything, no matter how little, that you do well or right. Like a gratitude list, but this is aimed only at yourself. Psychologist Dr. Beth Halbert calls it a brag list, and uses it to get her clients to begin to admit how awesome they really are. At first, this may feel hard, as we aren't used to listing what we do right, but rather, what we do wrong. Start with ten things that you are good at, or admire about yourself, and keep adding. If you add to your list every week and read through the list once a week or whenever you feel down, you will rewire some of your neural pathways to see your worth. Authors of *Code to Joy* explain that a practice like this works on our reticular activating system[8], or the neural network that filters every single piece of information we come across, to decide the relevance to us. Let it run wild, and your filter may not bring you information that supports you. Train it to focus on the good, and you build a muscle that helps you focus on the good.

No feat ranks too small. My list contains making great breakfasts, giving good hugs, and having a laugh others find contagious. Over time, reading through this list and cultivating the knowing that you are worthy will make it easier to step into greater visibility, confident that you can.

QUESTIONS FOR REFLECTION:

- Do you feel your worth on a day-to-day basis? Why, or why not?

- Does this support or hinder your business?

- If you don't always see your worth, what makes you think you are not worthy?

- Can you imagine changing that?

- Are you willing to try on some exercises or behaviors that could increase your feelings of worth?

6

GULP, A MARKETING PLAN?!

"Plans though well intentioned are not what you think they are. They are not a set of instructions for you to follow each day. Rather, they are a collection of intentions, hopes and possible actions that when fueled by love, can lead you to where you want to go." – channeled wisdom

Why they are confusing

L et's cut the mystique around this subject. Your marketing plan simply contains what you plan to do in your marketing efforts, where, who you'll do it with, and when you will do it. It's that simple. Now, the question may be if you can let it be that easy and find your own way. If you want to do your planning only once a year, go for it. Want to do it more often or only when it strikes you as time, I'm all for that. Want a formal written one, great. Plan to keep it on the back of a notebook cover? Fine. It's not so important how you do it as that you do it. And, not only for the sake of saying you did it.

You are looking for enough of a plan that you feel secure your actions are getting you somewhere. You want to know you've considered your business goals, who you are as a person, and what your resources are to create a good plan for yourself. Let's see how to do that with enough ease and grace that it's something you look forward to, rather than feel hopeless about.

Creating a solid plan will make you feel better instead of overwhelmed or afraid.

We all know how to plan. We do it every day. We plan for the next day by deciding on clothing, meetings, lunch, and maybe even what we'll do after work. We plan for holidays and birthdays—where we'll be, who's bringing what, and about what time. We plan with our vendors and clients to move their projects along. Sometimes, we even plan not to have any plans! In short, in today's society, we are all pretty much plan-making machines.

This makes it confusing when someone mentions a marketing plan to a small business owner and the only sound heard is crickets. The silence becomes uncomfortable while the entrepreneur squirms. It may seem funny when we read it that a grown person would squirm, but it doesn't feel funny in the moment.

Marketing plans are confusing for two main reasons:

1. The many ways you can reach clients via marketing makes it difficult to choose. Add to that, the pressure most entrepreneurs put on their marketing plan, i.e., it must be brilliant and successful. Marketing outcomes are not something you can know beforehand. This pressure can be unwarranted and unhelpful to the

planning process. That's like planning for a vacation while telling yourself the whole time this better be the best trip you've ever taken. Since you can't possibly control that, it's better to approach your vacation plan guided by your preferences and your resources, your intelligence, and your hopes. Same thing for your marketing plan.

2. Entrepreneurs don't like marketing plans because the goals they are trying to reach are often reached by at least some activities they dread. These activities are not in their comfort zone—but mostly because of limiting beliefs, such as "only sleazy sales people call potential clients" or "I don't have that skill set." Not doing a plan can simply be an avoidance mechanism. Their thinking goes something like this: It's not really avoiding if you haven't spelled it out on paper that you need to do it, right?

Darla is an entrepreneur who offers consulting to her clients. In the first three years of her business, she did a lot of networking, public speaking, and sought out referral sources to gain clients. Don't get lost in the jargon here, that's just saying that Darla spent a lot of her time meeting a lot of different people and developing relationships with them. She shared her expertise with them by giving talks at their meetings or in meeting them one-on-one. She did this organically, letting one person lead to another. This led to having enough clients for her small business to get started and pay for a simple lifestyle. She was thrilled the business was working. She loved learning the new skills of connecting people to each other, and enjoyed that she was becoming known in her area. It fit perfectly with her personality of helping others. She even started to like having a little recognition. Darla began to be confident in her skill-set with her clients. They were making progress in their businesses, and Darla got that she was part of that.

After the first three years, she began to feel restless and wanted to make more money. So, she set her sights on growing her business and serving more clients. However, as she researched different ways other consultants made more money in her industry, she was confronted with paths outside of her experience or skillset. Those who made more money either had longer/higher priced engagements with their clients, worked with groups of clients rather than individually, or had additional revenue streams beyond consulting, such as books, products, and online courses. She sought support around having longer/higher priced engagements with her clients, but was confronted with the fact that these engagements required different sales conversations than the ones she was used to. She needed to learn sales skills, and how to present the value of her higher priced packages. She would also need to consciously pursue clients, rather than just letting them seek her out. Instead of sitting down to create a plan and chart the steps needed—including learning new skills and doing more research—Darla chose to keep moving ahead in an organic way, taking whatever-comes approach. As a result, the additional revenue she hoped for has not manifested.

Instead, I hope you will be brave and face the parts of your plan you need to grow into. After all, that growth can lead you toward the desires you have for your business and your life. Isn't that worth it?

The following pages include several categories of information you need to gather to create your plan.

Be honest and find your heart's desire

Often, entrepreneurs focus on what they think they should do, such as obligations and best practices within your industry.

Yes, these are important, but your objectives should also be shaped by your real desires, hopes, and your personality. Trying to market something you don't really want to do or towards goals lacking meaning can be not only difficult, it doesn't get the best results.

How do you find your authentic desires and keep them realistic? Your state of mind matters here. You cannot dream into being that which you cannot imagine, or that which you feel you don't deserve. It can also be difficult to dream when you are tired, cranky, or feeling low. In those moments, you need to wait until you are in a better state so you can daydream, imagine, and think expansively.

It's easy to scale dreams back, but it's difficult to paint them larger when they start off small. So, go big in your thinking. Are you helping others make a difference in their lives? Are you making the world a better place in some way? Are you creating a career that helps you express yourself in a profound way? Or, are you doing all three? Follow your contribution all the way out to its greatest impact. Fill yourself with the possibilities for a different kind of world and your place within it.

Often, we think small because we are afraid our big dream may be out of reach or, worse, that we don't deserve it. Thinking this way overrides divine intelligence and the notion that we are created with a purpose. Who are you to question whether you should take this opportunity or keep yourself safe, rather than stretch to your full potential?

Some would say it's a sin to ignore the opportunities before you. At best, it may be your ego—or some version of temptation—to ignore your growth possibilities in favor of feeling safe or secure in material things. Even though virtually every spirituality and religion says to ignore the material in favor of the spiritual, this concept proves difficult for the Western mind. We are afraid of what we'll have to give up or the disruption we'll feel if we move toward our highest goal.

Remember, you are only dreaming at this point. This can help you around the fear. All journeys take a thousand steps to accomplish, so you'll only ever be asked to take the next step—not all the steps at once. This way, your risk stays quite small. You can tell yourself it's all on paper at this point, and you don't have to start if you don't want to! Our fears sometimes need to be coddled and held to quiet down, enough for us to move forward.

Once you have your larger dreams identified, celebrate! Then, move through the next few steps in this chapter before trying to use this information. This will ensure you are bringing in the practical means to enact it. I've noticed a lot of purpose-driven entrepreneurs carry around their dreams, as if writing them in their journal will bring them to fruition. In truth, you need to move to practical actions and sound guidance to accomplish them.

Create authentic objectives

Now that you have your larger dream identified, you must combine that with your goals for your business to lead you there. Do you have written objectives for where you are headed? Or, even know how you would identify them?

Your business goals should be specific and measurable, both so you can reach them and know when you've gotten there. They are usually about the money you'd like to earn, the impact you'd like to make, and the development of products/ services you need to do so.

How does that relate to your big dreams? Your desires are usually end-of-the-line items, such as being a published author, having a thriving business, or traveling the world doing your work. Imagine a staircase and your big dream sits at the top of the stairs. Your authentic objectives are the steps you're going to walk up to arrive at your dream. No one I know can stand at the bottom of the stairs and wish themselves to the top. You must make the effort to put one foot in front of the other and climb each step to get there. The upward steps are stages you must go through on your way, as your big dream may take years to accomplish. It could be two years away, five years away, or even more than 10 years. Each year, you'll have goals or objectives you need to reach to end up at that big dream someday.

For example, let's say your big dream is to have a small firm offering graphic design to clients around the country. Imagine this as the big goal at the top of the staircase. Let's look now from the bottom, leading up to this top point. Year one—or step one—you'll need to create your marketing materials such as a website, business card, and LinkedIn profile. You'll also need to find ways to become visible to potential clients through networking, or creating an online presence. And, you'll need to start landing jobs and executing them flawlessly.

Your objectives/goals for this first year might be written on your plan like this:

1. Create initial marketing materials (web, business card, online profile)

2. Sign up and attend six networking groups in the first three months; attend two regularly, for the rest of year.

3. Gain $3,000 in new business monthly for first three months; increase to $5,000 monthly for the rest of the year.

Those three goals will likely take you all your first year to reach, maybe more. They only support you; they are not enough to have a thriving small firm. So, you must keep going up the stairs.

Years two and three will be to continue with year one goals, removing goal one's start-up materials—though they will need regular updates—and adding the creation of systems for finances, marketing, and client servicing. You don't want to spend your time always doing the mundane things like balancing your books, paying invoices, creating client contracts, and answering emails. You want to create systems to handle routine things more quickly or automatically, so you have time to pursue new business. To keep business coming in, you might look to increase your visibility in your networking groups by taking on a volunteer position within the group, or taking on other kinds of new visibility. Finally, you look for ways to increase earnings enough to pay for staff beginning the next year, so you can meet that goal of being a firm, not a solopreneur.

So, year's two and three list might look like this:

1. Develop systems for ongoing finance management, marketing, and client servicing (describe each specifically with detail, for example, upgrade to QuickBooks, create auto scheduled monthly newsletter, and implement online contract signing for clients).

2. Increase visibility within networking group, or create new visibility avenue, that creates 20 new leads per month.

3. Identify and create strategy for pursuing new revenue stream or increase earnings of 30%.

Year four and five will have new goals meant to increase the types of jobs you are awarded, and the systems needed to support staff. Can you see how it might take five years before you have enough regular business and the base for your business to have staff? That might be only your first employee.

Of course, this holds if you are starting from scratch. Many people spin off of an existing job or skill set when starting a new business. In this example, if you were already doing graphic design for a company, you might spin off to your own business with a couple of good clients and hire a staff person right away. But, you'll still have those other objectives to meet over time, so you can expand. No matter where you start, you must break down your big dream into goals for the coming year, and then, break each of those goals down into monthly actions.

I prefer to call them objectives, rather than goals, for two reasons. First, the word goal can be uncomfortable for purpose-driven entrepreneurs. It's too corporate, too competitive, and too linear. Second, it's a good reminder to be objective, not emotional, about where you want to go. Sure, it's good to bring some emotion in, like how good it could feel to reach them, but you also must have some practical and actionable ideas about where you're going. You don't want to invite in the more negative type emotions like fear, doubt, and worry, as these are goal blockers.

Download a staircase worksheet here: lindabasso.com/reluctantmarketer

Admit your financial goals

Admitting your true financial goals can be hard for purpose-driven entrepreneurs who want to focus more on what they give than get. But giving more than what you have isn't sustainable. Undercharging or over-giving can cause resentment in the long run, and won't allow you to give your best service. Learn to receive gracefully, and remember the more you are given, the more you can give.

Or, it happens in the opposite way. A whole class of would-be entrepreneurs dream of making a ton of money with very little effort on their part. It's not that they don't want to help others or make an amazing contribution, they just also long for a life filled with financial ease and time for the things that make life matter. This culture's emphasis on money as the means to enjoy life fuels this type of daydreaming. The overwhelming amount of *earn seven figures fast* online programs for coaches, healers, and anyone who wants to sell their products/services online further complicates things.

Even those of us who are trained in business fall prey to this wildly swinging pendulum of financial hopes. Harder still to find realistic advice out there about starting a business, to know how much you need to spend, and when to expect realistic returns. When we do see information that's realistic, it seems so hopeless that we could truly make it. Instead, we may dismiss our dreams or secretly hope we'll be the exception.

One way we get these unrealistic ideas comes from what we hear about manifesting. Just visualize what you want! Of course, you can't have what you can't imagine, but you need more than vague notions of financial success. You must get very specific when it comes to money, both in naming what you need and planning for how to get it at various stages of your business.

Another way we veer off into dreamsville comes from the attention the media pays to instant millionaires. Ideas that go viral! High profile startups/buyouts! The internet is flooded with folks telling you they have the secret to six- and seven-figure business solutions. The amount of hype and exaggeration boggles the mind. We used to call them get-rich-quick scams, and warn people to avoid anyone who spoke in those terms. Remember the business of news means getting read, which it often accomplishes by focusing on the exciting, rather than the practical.

I've seen many entrepreneurs suffer under the pressure to perform at a financial level they are not yet capable of. Instead of guiding their businesses to unfold in a natural, sweet way, they push themselves to a lot of money, fast. This can undermine their confidence when their business doesn't produce as quickly as they want or need. They may begin to question their skill set or even if they should be in business at all. Have you ever felt like that? You may simply need more time, patience, and/or outreach. Rushing never gets you anywhere, except exhausted.

QUESTIONS FOR REFLECTION:

- How can you shift your focus from the fast and furious to the small, incremental, and joyful path that's needed to get a business up and running?

- How much time do you need in your schedule for planning and implementing these plans, in addition to serving clients?

- How can you be realistic about what you need to support yourself financially along the way?

Study the market

Learn about your competition. Many of my purpose-driven entrepreneur clients cringe when I tell them to study the market, but please, read this through before you jump to judgment.

It's common sense. You need to know the market, or industry, in which your product or service exists. Your business exists in a set of circumstances you should be intimately aware of to make a good plan. Your service should be timely, desired, and show an advantage to thrive.

How can you know more about the market containing your service or product? Remember those research papers you had to write in school? Apply the same concept. Research and read. Good news—unless you're writing a formal business plan, you are researching only for your own understanding, not to write a paper with citations. Have fun with this! If you can hold an attitude of excitement and joy around finding out how fascinating your industry might be, you'll get uplifted by immersing yourself in it. Even those who approach this with dread later tell me they became excited and proud to be part of their industry. It also helps you figure out how you are the same and different from others in your industry. Often, when my clients are studying their industry, or looking at their competition, they have ahas about themselves and their business. There's nothing like reading something about someone else and hearing your own agreement—or disagreement—with their position to create clarity for yourself.

How do you know what industry you are in? Sometimes, it's obvious. A lawyer is part of the legal industry, an accountant is within the financial industry, and a restaurant owner is part of the hospitality industry. Other times, you need to make some decisions about what you identify with. One health coach might identify more with the coaching industry, while another might lean toward the health/wellness industry, and still, another might choose to identify equally with both. Same thing for any consultant. If you are unsure, do a little online research to see what you can find, and ask other professionals until you find yours. Then read and research until you feel comfortable with your general knowledge of your industry.

Once you know the overall landscape of your industry, you need to look at others who offer to meet the same needs as you do. These are your competitors, but I mean that in the nicest sense of the word. I don't mean they are your rivals. Often, my clients resist this step because they don't like the idea that they are in a competitive situation, which usually connotes fiercely competing against one another, winners/losers, or trying to one-up each other. Feel free to use whatever word you like instead. Although, competitor literally just means another person or company who's offering a product or service like yours, you may prefer to label them colleagues, or something that doesn't make you afraid, overwhelmed, or bummed out.

Studying your competition can save you time and money, but only if you figure out 1) how you are the same as them, 2) how you are different, and 3) how to express this so others can understand. This is not a rhetorical exercise. You'll get asked all the time by potential customers how your service or product compares to another service or product that seems similar in their minds. That's the operative phrase: in their minds. Often, small business owners are so immersed in their own business; they take this distinction for granted. But, your potential customers are not immersed in your point of view. They are barraged with an amazing amount of information, and often must work very hard at understanding the best buying choice for themselves. That's why it's a great service for you to do the work of understanding how you compare to what's out there and explaining those differences honestly. You are helping buyers make a truly good choice for themselves.

Share the meaningful differences between you and your competition to be of service to potential clients.

We don't hesitate for two seconds to assess someone's outfit or talk about the people in our neighborhoods, companies, and families. We even have television shows based on this premise of looking at others' lives and comparing them to our own. How funny that in a society so set on comparisons, that we, small business owners, hesitate to look at our competition to make decisions because it seems like cheating. Small businesses are actually well served when they share information and grow from it. It moves the whole industry forward.

If you can drop the idea that it's copying and embrace the idea that nothing is original except your unique stamp on it, you'll experience more ease. Of course, I'm not talking about direct copying, which means plagiarism in writing, for example, but digesting another's approach, and making it your own. If it's helpful, please know that every famous artist, writer, or creative fills themselves with other's work to fuel their own inspiration and creative process. I went to art school and remember being amazed at how much time we took in class to study other's work. Sometimes, we even recreated another's work so we could get a glimpse into their process and choice making. By stepping into Picasso or Van Gogh's shoes—and literally trying to copy them—we students were turning on our own internal artistic decision-making while building the skill-set we would need to create our own masterpieces. Now, if we had tried to sell our copies, that would have been wrong. But, using them to propel our own process forward added to the world of artistic creations, as we were better prepared to make our own contributions. You can do the same by studying those around you who offer work that meets the same needs that you do.

I think this quote from famous filmmaker, Jim Jarmusch, sums it up nicely. And hey, if it's good for the famously creative, maybe there's something there for you, right?

Nothing is original. Steal from anywhere that resonates with inspiration or fuels your imagination. Devour old films, new films, music, books, paintings, photographs, poems, dreams, random conversations, architecture, bridges, street signs, trees, clouds, bodies of water, light and shadows. Select only things to steal from that speak directly to your soul. If you do this, your work (and theft) will be authentic. Authenticity is invaluable; originality is non-existent. And don't bother concealing your thievery – celebrate it if you feel like it. In any case, always remember what Jean-Luc Godard said: "It's not where you take things from – it's where you take them to. —Jim Jarmusch

My final thought on this is to ask you to broaden who you think of as competition. Notice above that I said others who meet the same needs as you do, not others who do the same thing as what you do. Why? Because, in today's economy, there are multiple ways to get the same needs met. Someone experiencing an illness 100 years ago in the U.S. could go to the local doctor or treat it at home. Now, in most places in the U.S., you can choose between a traditional or naturopathic doctor, a clinic, an herbalist, acupuncturist, or natural energy healer. There are multiple people whose different services could help you with your illness. In my business of marketing, there are consultants and coaches who specialize in marketing, along with business coaches and consultants who also deal with marketing—as well as books, online courses and workshops that all offer marketing help. To differentiate yourself effectively in the mind of your potential customer, you need to look at a variety of options they use, and understand how you are different and the same from each of them.

QUESTIONS FOR REFLECTION:

- Do you resist looking at your competition?

- Can you imagine learning and growing from doing so?

- How could you reframe this to be more positive if you find it distasteful?

- Could you use studying your competition as a way to energize your own approach?

7

BRING YOUR WHOLE SELF

Know your design

Personality, preferences, and the stage of life you are in should all be part of how you set up your marketing plan. I often see introverts struggling with marketing plans better suited for extroverts. Or, parents of young children wishing to launch a 6-figure business while being there for their children. Or, a retiree who on one hand, wants to slow down and on the other, start a new business for themselves. Am I saying these things can't be done? No, but I am saying these contradictions in life stage, personality, and preferences make the marketing efforts much more difficult. If you are willing to consider all of you in your planning, I find enacting the plan goes much more smoothly.

You should also consider the intangible design you were born with. Look to a typing system like Human Design, the Enneagram, Strengthsfinder, or another system to identify the individual way you were created. This ensures your plan takes full benefit of how you are designed. I like to use a car analogy with my clients. If you are designed to be a Porsche but you are moving through your life trying to do the heavy work of a diesel truck, or vice versa, you are probably not getting the best out of yourself, or the situations you are involved in. When you understand your unique design, you can take advantage of your inborn strengths, and bolster your weak spots.

Let's look at the Human Design system as an example. This system can help you understand the best way to network and get visible. A projector, one of the three types in the system that makes up only about 21% of the population, must be recognized by another, rather than approach someone directly. A generator type, which is 70% of us, must feel a pull or response toward someone before they can approach them. And a manifestor, which only describes 9% of people, can approach anyone, though they have better results if they inform others while they do it. There are, of course, many nuances in someone's Human Design chart I'm skipping here. I'm not trying to overly simplify this system, but am bubbling up the essence to make the point. The projector would do best at the event if someone else who knew them introduced them around. While the generator would be well served to hang back for a moment, and see who they had a response to before approaching anyone. The manifestor could approach anyone they like, although they would do best if they started off with letting the other person know, like "Hi, I'm stopping by to introduce myself, if that's ok." Since these three designs have vastly different approaches, to create a successful connection at the networking event, you would need to know your design.

It doesn't only make you more effective. It helps you bring your whole self to your marketing. We've moved past the time in our culture when it's ok to only bring a slice of yourself to your marketing efforts—to just say what you do. The transparency needed in today's marketing comes when you bring your whole self. Practically speaking, it comes when you bring your *why* into your marketing.

But we need to go beyond just the why of what we are doing. We need to fundamentally be ourselves. By this, I mean our real selves, not the false self we may have developed in defense to our hurts or our lack of acceptance of others. Back to our car analogy, if you were a diesel truck born into a family or culture of Porsches, you won't grow up feeling like that's a good thing. It's the proverbial ugly duckling story: the baby swan only feels beautiful in a group that doesn't come down on it for not being a duck.

At the core, it's not even about sharing your real self with others. How about the gift of getting to know your own self at an intimate level? The more you can accept yourself for who you really are, who you really came here to be, the more settled in your own skin you'll be. That quality attracts prospective clients.

Have you ever wondered how we got all these various typing systems here on earth? Some swear by their astrology, some by their Enneagram number, and others by their Strengthsfinder profile. In Ivy League graduate studies programs, students are required to assess themselves with the Meyers-Briggs or other personality team assessment tools. Corporations create their own tests or buy one of many types of enterprise level of assessments that include cognitive ability, personality, and even integrity tests. Outside consultants have built a plethora of their own systems such as Lance Secretan's 5Dynamics or Steve Faktor's Nine Corporate Personas. Carl Jung endorsed the channeled Human Design system, which set the stage for the Meyers Briggs system. The Enneagram can be traced through Sufi, Judaic, and Christian lineages. There are many types of assessments, and they come from various points of view, including intellectual, psychological, and even spiritual points of view.

How can all of these be right? How do you know which to use? From my perspective, each has something to offer, and it's about finding the one that resonates with you, in other words, that gives you understanding and helps you know more of yourself. Each person, who's created one of these systems, has seen a glimpse of the overall universal design, and created a system that brings to life some of the pieces, in ways that made sense to them. Some have divined the whole system, others have based it on observation. Neither ranks it as better or worse, and both have value. Something can be learned from each system that has been developed. If you try many systems, you should sense a thread among them that fits you.

Knowing your design and using it to make decisions comes in part because we have a society that doesn't value individuation. Culturally, we don't practice tools of self-inquiry in a way that leads to approaching the world through our own unique lens. Vision quests and coming-of-age rituals traditionally held this place, so a person might begin to know themselves deeply while still participating or finding a place within the tribe. Instead, in our consumer capital-based system, many of us have learned to fit in, rather than find our unique skill-set.

You must seek systems that feel resonant to you to understand yourself and your design. This is not a frivolous or self-indulgent thing. Knowing oneself used to be a high calling. People spent their lifetime trying to understand their own nature. Now we hurl ourselves forward so fast through time that we barely remember to breathe, let alone contemplate the deeper nature of ourselves.

Nor can you use the investigation of yourself as an avoidance mechanism or distraction. Many purpose-driven entrepreneurs keep learning more and more about themselves, seeking system after system. But it's really not to deeply know themselves, rather, it's looking for a quick fix or as a distraction from doing real growth work. It would be fine to explore some number of systems with the intent of finding the one or two you want to study and apply over time. In diving more deeply, you can gain true understanding of the real you. The goal of this exploration should not be to explain away your behavior, or to feel better about the things you do. It's to learn more about your own motivations, inklings, and weaknesses to be more accepting of yourself. This knowledge and acceptance create more alignment between you and the divine.

Say my guides:

You have a deep personal well of power, but may not realize it as you strive to fit in and be acceptable to others. For instance, some of you have the power of fighting the status quo, or of being individually oriented to learn about the human collective. This might cause some clash as our society dictates that we all be social. Your power may not feel like a power at all in the society in which you find yourself! Do not doubt how you were designed by the creator. You must go from the assumption that you were designed this way for a reason. Find it and act on it. This may be hard to understand but remember the world was not designed only for you. The creator seeks to understand all things about itself. This means there are many experiences you may want to reject personally, but are meaningful as energy or experience.

We've also come to believe that we can change ourselves or become a better version of who we are. Nothing could be further from the truth, and this pursuit will cause you great pain as you deny your very nature in favor of fashion or outside opinion. You must find the systems you have resonance with, study them, apply them to your lives, all with the focus of finding the real parts of you. Finding unsavory parts or difficult parts may not feel easy, but this path doesn't promise ease. You must learn to admit truth even when it seems painful to do so. It can be much more painful to suppress it. Admitting it only stings in the beginning and then, gets integrated into your strength of being.

I know because I've been on this journey myself. I've studied many systems and learned a great deal about myself, both good and bad. At one point, I learned from studying Claudio Naranjo, a Chilean psychologist who presented an interpretation of the Enneagram, that I am vain, selfish, and cruel. Was this easy for me to really admit? Heck no, even though I know deep down I really do have these qualities as part of me. It was heartbreaking as I really have spent a good part of my life trying so hard to be good. It still causes me to feel uncomfortable, and I don't go out of my way to dwell on it for sure! But somehow, I can say I am also stronger for knowing this. It gives me a depth that people respond to. I'm often told how real I seem. It is also humbling for me, and helps me more quickly resolve situations when any of these traits come to the surface. Because I'm not in denial of them, it's easier for me to see them and admit them so they pass through, rather than causing a lot of drama. I have much more control of them than I would if I was suppressing them.

Being honest about your shortcomings does not make them stronger, as many fear. It's not in naming your weaknesses that they grow. Instead, when you admit them, it puts you in a conscious relationship over them—one that gives you more choice and greater control of your actions.

The better you can come to know yourself, the more of you that can truly show up in your business. It makes it easier to create a realistic plan for yourself and your business. By considering the real you, there's a better chance your plan will be realistic to what you can do.

Find your resources

You are creating a marketing plan for your business—not a list detailing dozens of marketing activities you must enact by yourself. Too often, that's exactly how it feels, which can be a lonely and limited position.

Instead, you can look to all the resources available to you. Stretch beyond your own personal skill sets or resources, which can only deliver a business you alone create. Instead, imagine what you could do with the right strategic partnerships, or resources above and beyond yours. Increase the impact you make by becoming a part of a larger professional community. Think about how you can tap into your spiritual traditions to accomplish more. Don't feel like your business is all on you. It's not.

Your plan doesn't only involve you and your customers. In truth, your business came here to do something beyond you. Yes, it's your business, and maybe it's being run by you. Or maybe you are the inventor of/or main service provider in it. Yes, it's terribly personal, but it's not really all about you. You and your business are separate entities; each with your own energy and desires.

Your marketing plan should name where your business wants to go in terms of visibility. Your job is finding the resources—money, people, opportunities—for it to have that level of visibility. This takes the situation out of the limited *I* of the business person, and into the greatest potential of the business.

Your marketing plan is to go where you business wants to go, it's your role to take you both there.

What if you and your business have different ideas about what kind of visibility your business should have? In my experience, it's best to let the business guide this. We tend to cloud our marketing plans with hopes, fears, and what we believe our financial needs to be. Our business usually has a clearer vision that's connected to our divine path. In truth, we are all here on a spiritual journey and often, our entrepreneurial activities are part of that spiritual ride, rather than the material one. Most of us can't get over our human thoughts about money when it comes to our business.

Even if it seems like there's a difference, more often than not, the entrepreneur's view on visibility and their businesses views on visibility come together at some point. Great, now you both want the same thing! It's usually only the timing that is different. Either the business wants a high level of visibility that seems scary for the entrepreneur at this time of their life, or the business wants to coast along at a time the entrepreneur believes it should be growing. I believe you'd do well to follow the lead of your business and trust in a higher divine order at play, even if it seems personally uncomfortable.

Besides, we don't always see what's happening at the time it's happening. Have you ever experienced a period in your life that seemed fallow or stagnant, only later to realize you were gaining the exact skill set you needed in order to take a giant step forward in your life?

Nancy was an art buyer, who had great skill in her craft, and whose clients loved her work. But the projects were not coming in routinely enough for her business to feel stable. She experienced times of overwhelm when she had too many projects, and fear when there was too little work, causing her to scramble for more. Although she loved her business, she longed for it to grow into something both comfortable to her schedule and financial needs. Then she was invited to bid for a bigger project than she had yet had. This meant she had to hire some outside help to put the proposal together, and assemble a larger internal team than she was used to putting on her projects. Then, during the process of bidding for this job, her admin person let her know she was going to quit, one of the consultants she brought in for the internal team fainted during the proposal presentation and had to go to the hospital, and Nancy herself got into a car accident. To top it off, she wasn't awarded the large job.

Although this seemed like just the opposite of what she needed, it started her down the path of getting to the business she wanted. In the aftermath of everything that had happened, Nancy had to take back the tasks her admin was doing, and set them up in a way that worked for her, rather than how her assistant had wanted to do them. She began learning every aspect of her business. In doing so, she realized she could do more if she upgraded her project management skills. So she took a course to become certified in this. She hired a bookkeeper and set up internal systems. Her business became more solid and streamlined. When she realized she was uncomfortable with creating relationships with strangers, she started attending more networking and social events. Taking this small risk over and over, she became more comfortable with her own value, and how she is received by others. She went through every aspect of her professional and personal finances, cutting and organizing until she felt comfortable with what was coming in and going out. She could now discuss them and make decisions around them. Although she didn't have enough work coming in, and the future of her business was uncertain, Nancy focused on getting comfortable with the reality of her current business, her skill set, and her desires for more business. This led her to find the courage to invest money in her business, hire outside help to refresh her website, and pursue new business opportunities, rather than waiting for them to find her. A few months later, Nancy had not only enough business again, but more than she'd had the year before. The biggest difference was Nancy achieved what she'd longed for—a business that was both comfortable to her schedule and financial needs. She now feels comfortable with the notion that she can continue getting new business at a pace supportive to her because her business is set up to do that.

Did Nancy do all of this consciously? Not really. As these events were unfolding, she couldn't really see things were headed toward a good end. Did she love taking back the admin tasks, hiring a bookkeeper, or setting up new internal systems? Nope. But, it seemed like the only reasonable choice. She could pack it all up, citing bad luck as a cause for her business failing, or take a step in a direction that felt personally uncomfortable. By showing up and taking the next step her business was asking her to take even though she didn't always love it, she lived her way into a more solid, confident version of herself and, hence, her business.

What step is your business asking you to take? Are you willing to take it and trust the higher order that might be at play? Or, are you sitting in your version of what should happen and asking your business, and perhaps, even the world, to shift around you? I see entrepreneurs doing both, though only one of these paths reliably works in the long run.

Just how do you find what level of visibility your business wants? Simply put, just ask! That's right; your business loves to share its viewpoints and ideas with you, if you ask it. Since most of us aren't exactly in the habit of chatting it up with our businesses daily, here are a couple of tips on how to get in contact with your businesses point of view.

1. **Free writing:** You've heard of stream of consciousness writing where you put your pen down on the paper and don't lift it for some period to get to the deeper wisdom you are holding inside yourself. You can use this same concept to get in touch with your business. It's helpful if you make a pleasant setting for yourself, perhaps in nature, or lighting a candle at your desk, or finding another beautiful setting to write in. This signals a special or sacred time. Take a few breaths and let go of any need to be in control or any fears you have about receiving new information. It's helpful if you can set aside any thoughts you have, and write from a state of innocent curiosity. If you try to write from an anxious, controlling place, you will have a harder time. Choose

the amount of time you are willing to write. I find 10 minutes to be a minimum, but over 20 minutes to be tiring. You can experiment to see what works for you. Ask yourself what your business has to say to you. Set the timer, then put your pen on the paper or hands on the keyboard, and write anything that comes up in your mind. I mean anything, so long as you don't stop writing. If you start thinking about the laundry, ask yourself what your business perspective might be on that and write it. If you are thinking how silly this effort seems, ask your business what it has to say about that. Try to accept anything that comes up, and get it all out on paper with the hope that you can begin to have a dialogue with your business. It might take a time or two of trying before your business (or the part of you that can tap into the spirit of your business) feels safe enough to say something real. After all, you've likely been ignoring it for some number of years now.

2. **Visualization:** The following is a visualization I created to tap into the same information. If you prefer to listen to it, either read through it while recording it and play it back for yourself, or download it here: lindabasso.com/reluctantmarketer

Find a comfortable seated position. Feel the surface beneath your legs, what your feet are touching, and notice the position of your back. Lengthen through your spine so your head and neck come over your hips, without your head or your shoulders slumping forward. Resting comfortably, imagine a golden light surrounding you, bringing you a deep sense of peace and acceptance. Breathe in this light, letting it infuse every cell in your body. Bathed in this loving light, imagine your business is now sitting across from you in its own chair. For even though your business seems to be yours, and may be of you, it is also separate from you. Your business has come to be in this time with its own agenda, its own ideas, and its own contribution that it wants to make. You are in partnership together on this journey. If you can approach a conversation with your business with curiosity and non-judgment, it can share with you what it needs to grow or make the contribution it wants to. First, ask your business what contribution it wants to focus on making in the coming year. Or, you can ask about next week. Pick a time you are curious about. Listen as your business tells you or shows you pictures, or communicates in some way to you about the contribution it wants to make, and by whom this contribution is being received. [pause] If you didn't receive anything, relax and be willing to allow this information to come in. Take whatever comes without judging it. Or, trust that it will reveal itself at another time. Now, ask your business what level of visibility it wants to have to be able to make this contribution. Again, listen to what your business has to say, or the pictures it shows you, or however it wants to communicate this information to you. Allow the information to unfold naturally and easily. Perhaps you have a small level of visibility, only working with a limited number of people. If so, know that it is totally fine. Or perhaps, you see yourself working with hundreds of people over the life of your business. Maybe thousands. Whatever you see or hear, know that all's well. [pause] If you notice any discomfort in yourself in receiving this information, be willing to set it aside for now. This can be dealt with at another time. When your business has shared the visibility it desires with you, thank it for sharing. Let it know that you will visit it regularly, to check in and share information. Become aware of your physical body again. Your feet on the floor, your legs on the chair, and the position of your back. Come out of the visualization slowly, and open your eyes when ready.

Now that you have an idea of the kind of visibility your business desires, it's up to you to support it. If you are responsible for creating the visibility your business wants, just how do you find the resources for that? You need to tap into resources beyond the financial ones you need to have in place to enact your plan. Look at the people you know, the networks you are part of, vendors available to you, and even technology solutions. Yes, getting your business going in the right direction rests a lot on you, but not totally. Any successful person has a slew of people behind them supporting them.

It's helpful if you create clarity for yourself, as most people are amazed by the amount of resources they really have in their lives. Go through the list below and note what you have resources for and what you do not. You want to know what support you have, and what may be missing to move forward gracefully.

What if you are lacking support in one or more areas? No problem! In coaching, we call this upgrading your network. It means you consciously seek out anything missing from your professional resource pool, so you have the right support in order to reach your business goals. That does not mean you're going to gain all the skills that are lacking for yourself. Let me repeat: this does not mean you are adding a long list of skills you must learn to your to-do list. It does mean making connections with the people who can provide them, or can refer you to those who can. A strong professional network means you can get done what you need to get done by resourcing from trusted professionals you've gathered around you.

No one moves forward without support behind them.

Having a strong professional network can be the lifeblood of your business. When you see business owners who get most of their work by referral, you are likely looking at a business owner with a strong network of connections around them. We still live in an economy of people who choose to work with people they like and trust. Trust comes from nurturing strong relationships. It's not just about getting business, though. It's also about better serving your clients. When you are a well-connected person, you have the possibility of helping your clients get whatever they need to be successful. When you can refer a client to a vendor to help them in their personal or professional life, or another person who can help them in some way, you are being of service to them.

Here's a list of categories to review on the amount of resource in your life. Put a check mark in two places—whether you have it or don't, and then whether it has to come from you or you can outsource it to another person. Download a printable version here: lindabasso.com/reluctantmarketer

	Have	Don't have	Has to be you	Need someone

YOUR SELF
ideas for your business
strengths to enact ideas
personal talents & skills
health & energy
appearance/clothing

PHYSICAL
office or place to work
storage or filing places
equipment (like a massage table or other)
a well-ordered home to support your off time

SPIRITUAL
self-practice
sacred spaces
natural places

NETWORK
professional connections _____
greater community _____
ongoing opportunities to meet new people _____

RELATIONSHIPS
family harmony _____
close friends _____
close colleagues _____

FINANCE
budgeting skills _____
money-tracking system _____
cash-flow understanding _____
review time _____
comfort with earning money _____
invoicing system _____
bill-paying system _____
credit to get you through tight cash flow _____
savings to support you through downtimes _____

TECHNOLOGY
equipment (computer, etc.) _____
writing/editing software (like Word) _____
presentation software (like PowerPoint) _____
systems to support business functions
(appointment software, calendar, online ordering, etc.) ___
website _____
LinkedIn profile _____
Facebook & other social media _____

Voila! Go back through the list and for anything you checked "don't have," you now know something you need to begin developing as a resource for your business. Here are ways you can expand your resource pool:

1. First, use the previous list to determine what kind of upgrades you need to make, rather than those that could have someone else to do it. Then, plan to get that upgrade into your life. If it's a skill-building upgrade, like learning a new software or how to budget, and you determine that you need this skill upgrade, ask around for classes, books, or teachers who can help you gain these skills— or look online. Set aside time in your schedule to learn the skills or make the upgrades that you need to make.

2. If you have upgrades that someone else can make for you, get busy hiring them. For example, maybe you want to dress more professionally or expand your creativity, so look for a coach or stylist who can help you achieve this. Or maybe you need to hire someone to create some systems for you.

3. If you need to expand your network so you know more vendors or have more professional contacts, seek out appropriate networking groups. You can find them via online searches, through your Chamber of Commerce, or through Meetup.com. Some are drop-in groups you can go to now and then. Others require a weekly commitment. All of them let you visit a couple of times before you make any decisions. If you don't find a group near you, consider starting one! I've known several entrepreneurs who increased their business by starting their own networking group.

   Your networking does not have to be limited to physical groups, although I recommend that every entrepreneur have strong ties to their community. You can participate in online networking in a couple of ways. One is through LinkedIn, which is an online network for the most part. I say for the most part, because in truth, LinkedIn works best when we only invite in professionals we know in person when we start our profile, and regularly add new professionals we meet out in the physical world. Knowing each of your connections personally means you have a know-like-trust factor with them, and are more likely to respond to each other if a need arises. Everyone hates to have a stranger invite them in to their circle only to have them start trying to sell them something! Likewise, when a friend or colleague of ours reaches out to be introduced to someone, we are usually too happy to help. Create a profile, and invite every professional contact you personally know to connect with you via LinkedIn. Remember, these should be people you personally have met, otherwise, it won't be effective. You can then interact with people in your LinkedIn network the same way you would in your physical networking groups. Say congratulations to them when they experience work success, send them an interesting article you just read, and regularly publish articles on your own expertise. Your goal should be to create the same level of visibility within your group as you might within your physical networking groups. LinkedIn then makes it easy to reach out to your network—and beyond—when you want to be introduced to someone or need something specific. For example, if you are doing research for a new service you're creating, you could search for people to have an informational interview with. When you find an ideal person, you can see if any of your connections are connected to that person so they can facilitate a direct introduction to that person.

4. Another way you can network online comes from joining various Facebook groups that have your ideal clients in them, or are filled with the types of professionals you need to know. By regularly commenting and sharing within these groups, you can create online connections similar to how you might create personal ones.

Now that you've created the awareness of what you need, be on the lookout for the universe to send it your way. This means be out and about! Talk to people sitting next to you in the café or at the gym. Ask people questions when they seem to have what you are seeking. There's a world of resource around you if you are open to it coming to you. You can also use online searches and read books or articles to know more about topics you need to be savvy about. This rarely gets entirely solved while you sit in your office. Get involved in the world around you, and experience the amazing synchronicities that unfold.

Ask the right people

I get asked questions by entrepreneurs all the time. Politely, I point out that I could give my opinion but that, unless I fit the profile of their perfect client, I might not be the right person to answer their question. Most pause as they consider my subtle clue, but choose to pursue their question anyway. We are often so hungry for advice in the beginning of our businesses that we ask anyone. Later, we are so wary of having received so much wrong input that we don't ask enough. Instead, try to find a balance of taking in and making your own way—and developing the discernment to know the difference.

Be sure to ask for input only from experts who jibe with your ideas about what a successful business really looks like, and/or have ideologies and perspectives you respect. Often, entrepreneurs take advice from anyone who's successful, only to discover the way that person earned their success doesn't match how the entrepreneurs work. That experience becomes one of those learning experiences we all have had along the way. Or, when we're having a bad day, reframed as wasted time and money.

I remember studying with one business coach for almost a year before realizing the model she taught was not one I ever wanted to have in my business. I went all the way through her program, even enacted a lot of what she taught with success. It wasn't until I sat down and mapped out how the next two years of my business would be if I used her model that I realized how unhappy I would be having that kind of business. Additionally, I realized over that year how hard she was working, and what her business required of her just to keep up. Although she had skills valuable to me, she was not the right person to help me take my business where I wanted it to go because she had no experience with the kind of business I wanted to have. Since then, I've chosen my teachers, mentors, and coaches with more care and understanding of what they could teach me, and how that plugs into growing my business.

It's important that you are careful about both the kind of people and the kind of advice you look for. When you think about your own business and where you want it to end up, ask yourself:

- Do you have the right people around you to give you advice?

- Are the teachers and mentors in your world running businesses you admire, both in the service they provide and how they market it?

- Do you like the lifestyle they have?

- Do you agree with their ethics and approach?

- Do you hire coaches because they can teach you a specific skill you've already determined you need or because you got excited by their inspiring speech at a conference?

Asking people who fit the profile of your ideal client can be another great way to get feedback pertinent to your product or service, your marketing, how you deliver it, and how your customer service comes across.

I don't mean asking your current clients, even if they fit the description of your ideal client. You are already in a relationship with them, and they already hired you. This means they've passed the psychological barrier of deciding you are a fit for them, so their input will tend to be biased toward understanding your messaging. In other words, they aren't very helpful in helping you get new people in! Speaking with folks who fit the profile of your client but are not your client can be a simple way to get input on how your messages are being understood, what their needs and hopes are, how they take in information, and what their current beliefs are about your industry.

What kinds of things do you ask them? Well, start by using them as a testing ground. If you are writing an ebook, have a few testers read it and answer a couple of questions, such as what they learned from it, if it made them want to know more, and if it inspired them to take next steps with your work (in other words, follow the call to action I know you put at the end of your ebook!). If you're launching a new service or product, interview a few people before you finalize it to be sure you're building a product/service meeting their needs. Later, have a few use it and share their feedback about what they liked and didn't like.

Any marketing messages you write can be shared with these folks before you launch them to your greater audience. Finding out beforehand whether your marketing creates a response or not, sure beats sending out your campaign messages only to hear crickets in response. Ditto for delivery and customer service. Getting comments on how that experience came across for testers and making adjustments feels better than hearing from a customer who's had a bad experience. Using people who fit *your* ideal client profile to preview your materials will help you be sure that what you are creating will be well received.

Of course, I'm not saying you should never ask your actual customers for their input. I encourage you to elicit feedback several times during your interactions with customers to be sure things are on the right track and they are happy. Also, ask them for a testimonial about their experience with you for use in your marketing materials. Ask them to review their experience via a survey or by answering a few questions when you finish working with them. This kind of information gathering will help you make the needed adjustments to your business so it continues to flourish.

In the end ... a plan

If you've taken in the information in this section, then you know all you need to create a plan in your own way. You have identified your larger dream, your authentic goals, and named the amount you need to earn. You're aware of yourself, and know the resources you have, as well as the ones you need to find. You've studied the market and gotten input from the right people.

Once you gather all this information, what do you do with it? It's time to move from gathering it to incorporating it into your plan. You'll need to analyze the information you receive, and use it to make decisions that are in alignment with your business goals. All the information either gets rejected or incorporated. And if it's included, that means acting on it. Too often, I meet entrepreneurs who've been busy gathering information from various experts and customers—but never enact any of it. If your clients are giving you feedback that they want something from you, find a way to give it to them. If you seek an expert's advice, decide whether you should act on it and, if so, find the courage to do it.

When you've done your research, you have all the information you need for your plan. If you've been drawing conclusions about all the information you've been gathering, you can already see that. If not, carve out some time to reflect on what you've learned about each of these areas. Pencil out your reflections into a plan or paint them into a visual rendition. Or, sticky note them all over your wall. It's not important what format you use. Remember, a marketing plan is like all the other plans you make in your life. It's simply what you're going to do, at what time, and with who to end up where you want to be. If you still cannot see what your plan could be, talk with someone who can help you organize your thoughts. You just might need some help in crafting your plan into a digestible format.

Your plan can be as simple as jotting down a few notes about what you are going to do and when on a single piece of paper. Or, if you prefer, make it more elaborate. There's no shortage of templates on the internet. If you are a visual person, you can create a collage or piece of art reflecting on the information you've gathered—from a single vision board-style plan to an elaborate collaged notebook or box. There's no limit to how you can put your plan together, nor is there any right way. The formal business plans of many pages you've likely read about are primarily for companies needing to pitch investors for funding. If you aren't looking for funding, then you can do whatever you'd like. Caution: be sure it's practical to your business, reflects your personality, and seems easy to use. Why do all that planning and toss it into a drawer? Choose a format you can use often, review every quarter, and update easily. I use a one-page plan with my clients, download it here: lindabasso.com/reluctantmarketer

CONCLUSION

To have the things we truly want, we have to grow. I wish it were different, that we could simply dream our perfect business and home life into being, but I've yet to see that happen. It takes courage, openness, determination, and action. The best laid plans never come to be if they don't get acted on. Am I right? How many times have you intended to do something, or longed to do something, or seriously wanted something to change but you didn't actually get to the acting part—and it never happened?

I know as I've been there. My first career lasted 21 years, and I didn't love it. All along the way, I wanted to make a change but I just couldn't see how. Good news for me in that, even though I wasn't yet making a change, I was doing some of the work in this book. Finding my truth, sussing out my purpose, and breaking family ties. That laid the groundwork so when I finally saw my real opportunity—to reach thousands of entrepreneurs through my writing and speaking—I was finally able to start acting.

Now, powerful actions are part of my everyday vocabulary.

That doesn't mean my days are filled with only sunshine and roses. I constantly find ways to inspire myself, take actions when I'd rather not, and support myself through fears and doubts. Because here's the rub: no matter how far you've come, there's somewhere up ahead beckoning you to come further still. And then, the whole journey starts over again.

The trick is to learn to dance with cycles of wanting, growing, having, wanting more, and doing it again. I've learned that small, steady steps toward change are better than a big leap resulting in a lot of stress, and gives you nothing but thoughts of giving up. I hope this book will help you in this. Now that you've read it through, go back and pick an issue to move along a bit more. If you did only some of the exercises, do a few more. Take a look at your business, and be honest about where you are struggling. Use the advice in this book to address this area directly. On any given day, open the book randomly, and see if the message applies to a situation within your business.

Steady, small steps forward add up over time to be big, lasting accomplishments.

For effective change, you may need to live into some of this material, then revisit it and have a new experience. You may find yourself drawn to new paths of exploration, or to dive more deeply into a concept. Again, trust your path. There's no exact formula for marketing, for business, or really, for life. There's only the process of it unfolding, and our decision to be conscious and engaged with the process.

Be kind to yourself along the way. I've made many significant changes in my life but if I'm honest, the ones that stick are the ones that unfolded over a long period of time with small, subtle changes that added up over time to be a big change.

If nothing else, I hope this book has uplifted your thinking around marketing. In my heart of hearts, I hope a little more for you. Step further into your truth. Or, out of your comfort zone and into a plan that's full of opportunity. Maybe that it will cut some old ties and give you a fresh perspective on being visible. And that, all in all, you can bring your whole self to your business.

Which, in the end, reduces your reluctance.

Isn't that the point? We know we have to either keep going, or pack it in and give up. It's simply not possible to just sit in the middle for any great length of time. If we can find tools for moving forward with more grace and ease, we can loosen up our reluctance and enjoy the ride.

Good thing you don't have to go it alone. When you partner with the divine in this journey, you're held by an indescribable grace. You get just the right amount of push, as well as the gentle hand of slowing you down, and all on an as-needed basis. If you believe something bigger than you holds the overall picture, you can relax into your current piece with more ease. You can breathe a sigh of relief knowing it's not all up to you. You can step into this amazing opportunity we have as humans, to bring the divine to life right here on planet earth. There's no better place to do that than in your business.

You don't even need to wonder how exactly you need to grow. I've seen many entrepreneurs pursuing endless growth programs, hoping they'll gain enough self-confidence, enough skill, or enough of something they lack that will ensure success. But in truth, the right growth for you will come as you start to act in your business. It's a magic formula.

There's no amount of getting ready you can do before acting in your business that will make sure it all works out. You learn by doing it.

The exact actions and growth we need are pointed out by stepping forward. There's truly no marketing formula or specific advice I can offer that's better than this—move forward in your business, trusting that will be asked to grow in just the right way to ensure your success. I've seen this work so often I've stopped being surprised. I still feel awed by the miracle every time my clients grow to their next level.

The exact growth you need to excel in your business comes up as soon as you step forward—but not before.

In the process, you'll learn some of what makes you tick. You'll accept more, and more, of who you really are. Knowing yourself brings you one of the most precious gifts you could receive. Once you accept where and who you are, you are freed up to rejoice in what a fabulous creation you are. That's when the fun starts.

It all comes back to this one idea—grow yourself, grow your business.

What's next?

The original channeling for this book contained the information I shared in this book, plus much more. In the first three months, I received about 20,000 words of channeled material. By the time I explained all the concepts, added in examples and exercises, it grew to 110,000. Which by a modern-day reader's standards, is simply too long. Plus, marketing is a subject that can feel overwhelming all too easily. Having a thick, heavy book just didn't feel right.

After some furious head scratching, my editorial team—which of course included some divine guides—and I decided to break the material up. Suddenly, I was publishing not one, but three books. So, consider passing along your copy of this first book to a fellow entrepreneur who might grow from reading it, and dive into the second and third book of *The Reluctant Marketer series*.

In these other two books, you'll learn how to love and laugh your way through marketing. With spiritual grace, rather than only pursuing an endless to do list, your marketing journey can be uplifting and supportive of making a real contribution in your work.

The first book, *Love*, shows that when you offer your business efforts to something higher than yourself, you bring divine power to your approach. Rather than putting your marketing out in the traditional push way, love demands you to create resonance and divine timing within your marketing instead. Love asks you to release resistance with blessings, and become the creator you were meant to be. By truly hearing the stirrings of your own heart, releasing the drama of human life and getting to know yourself, you are one step closer to this path. There are questions for reflection, exercises, and instructions for rituals included.

The second book, *Laugh*, takes you on a different path. Here, we see how laughter is powerful. It heals and helps us to live better lives. So, why not choose laughter over hard work? Then, you can bring play into your marketing, which brings ease—and better results. This new lightness lets you step into flow within your business and your marketing, learning to experiment and refine your way to marketing success.

You don't have to do it all alone. Not only can you access your divine guidance on this journey, you can also join other like-minded entrepreneurs. Believe me that it's easier when we see that others are on a similar path. Too often, we feel like the reluctance is only happening to us. I promise you it's not. Come join my community at lindabasso.com/reluctantmarketer. Together, we can do this so much more easily than each of us on our own.

Because in the end, this is just one step in the journey. When you speak with successful entrepreneurs, they tell you about the thousands of steps they've taken to reach where they are. As spiritual beings, we are all in a process that takes our entire lives to live out. Along the way, we become more and more of our best selves. Which means we have more to contribute to others who may be just behind us on the path. So go on, get out there and grow yourself, so you can share it with the world. I'll be right beside you doing the same.

WORLD RELIGIONS & SPIRITUAL PRACTICES MEET MARKETING

What could Buddha or Jesus possibly have to do with your marketing? I've studied and researched many world religions and spiritual approaches, searching for how they can inform our marketing. I am not a scholar of religions, but I have learned how the grace that unfolds from a religious practice is helpful to me and my clients. In this chapter, I've covered these paths and how they can inform marketing. This will help you start to translate for yourself what spiritual truths exist that can be overlaid onto your marketing experience. Because, isn't that the point? No religion or spiritual approach can tell us how to behave in every situation. Rather, it's the meaning we draw from the teachings, and how we enact it in our daily lives, that brings the teaching to life.

Am I suggesting you pick and choose from these to support you in your marketing? Not really, though I know that will work for some readers. In an ideal world, you'd dig deeply into one brand of faith and all the advice or teachings it has on your business life. In drawing the parallels I see in each, I am trying to illustrate that there is no business left behind in any religion or spiritual approach. These two do not have to remain separate.

Generally, there are twelve world religions considered to be classic: Baha'i, Buddhism, Christianity, Confucianism, Hinduism, Islam, Jainism, Judaism, Shinto, Sikhism, Taoism, and Zoroastrianism. I admit I was as surprised as you are to see some of these! Growing up in the Midwest, I was exposed to only a handful on this list. Moving to the Bay Area in my early twenties, added a couple more. In my mid-forties while doing this book research, five were still unknown to me. This illustrates how the part of the world you live in, and what you are surrounded by, has everything to do with the kind of information you are exposed to. That may mean the piece of information you need to make your own shift is in another part of the world, or in a non-formal religion.

I've added to this list several spiritual approaches, like Paganism, Indigenous, and Spiritual But Not Religious. Hopefully, these cover any reader who's not affiliated with an organized religion. Let's explore this alphabetically arranged list, and see what we can learn.

Baha'i

The Baha'i religion believes there is one unified God who is known by the world through a variety of prophets. These prophets are the founders of other religions such as Buddha, Christ, and Mohammed, as well as Baha'u'llah, who founded Baha'i in 1863. This makes it the world's youngest classic religion.

A fundamental teaching of Baha'u'llah is the oneness of humanity. There is an open rejection of racism, classism, nationalism, and gender inequalities. It was the goal of Baha'u'llah to create a world full of equality for men and women, all classes and races. He says, "Ye are all leaves of one tree and the fruits of one branch." Humanity is like a tree, with nations or peoples as the branches, and individual humans are the leaves. We're all part of the same tree. Sounds good, right?

I so long for entrepreneurs to feel this way about their business! Think of it as one tree, with the branches being your clients, vendors, and all the parts of your business—finance, operations, sales, and yes, marketing. The leaves are all the ideas, tasks, and care needed for each branch to be full and vibrant. You must tend to the whole tree as a unit, and care for each of the branches separately for the tree to do well. Can you imagine a tree where the gardener took loving care of one branch while feeling dread about the other ones, and only giving them attention occasionally? That's what I often see purpose-driven entrepreneurs doing when they are pouring all their attention on their client branch, dreading their marketing and sales branches, and only doing the bare minimum on their finances and operations.

There's a deeper instruction here as well. Run a business that contributes to the unity of humanity. Does your product or service help with class, gender, or race inequalities? Good. Empower others to step into their highest selves? You're on the right track. The Baha'i would have you use your business to pour out love, compassion, and unity to the world.

The Baha'i faith believes each person has their own relationship with God. We have eyes and ears—and the gift of reason—to recognize truth for ourselves. We are not meant to live our lives through the eyes or ears of another. This gives us all a high level of personal responsibility: to know God, follow his creative plan for us, do work that is useful to society, and to seek moral and work education that supports us in doing that.

With Baha'i adherents, education in trades and morality is compulsory. The Baha'i teachings promote moral and spiritual education, in addition to arts, trades, sciences, and professions. The emphasis on education is a means for the improvement of nations, and ultimately, the world. This helps the Baha'is in their duty to do work useful to humanity.

If you're a successful entrepreneur, chances are you are already doing both these things—taking a high level of personal responsibility for your path and getting ongoing training you need, both professionally and personally, to do so. If that training is addressing you spiritually as well, I believe that you and your business will soar. I've met many successful people who wonder if success is all there is, and why they worked so hard to get there. Rarely is that person spiritually fulfilled. Likewise, I've met many who are spiritually fulfilled, but materially longing for their needs and comforts to be met. Why not combine these for the best of both worlds?

On the topic of seeing things both ways, since the Baha'i see religions as progressive, and theirs as the latest progression, there is no conflict between religion and science in this faith. Abdu'l-Baha, the son of the Baha'i prophet and living embodiment of the faith, said religion must conform to science and reason, otherwise, it is superstition. The Baha'i believe God created man with the mind, or reason, to discover truth. Therefore, scientific knowledge and religious belief must be conformable to the analysis of this divine faculty in man. This aids in meeting the goal God had for creating humanity—that each of us would come to know and love Him.

I love this earthly, rational approach to the divine. You could be well served by bringing this into your marketing: a bit of divine guidance, mixed with practical realism in your business is a recipe for success.

Buddhism

Buddhism is an ancient philosophical system that follows the teachings of the Buddha. The system — a meditative, esoteric practice that often functions as a religious system — has an estimated 350 and 500 million practitioners and believers, worldwide. Buddhism emphasizes the cultivation of mindfulness, and values a spiritually minimalistic worldview, eschewing dependence and worldly attachment. Different schools of Buddhism emphasize different aspects of the tradition. Some focus on the practice of Samadhi, or meditation and mental development, and Prajna which is the discernment, insight, and wisdom that will emerge if your mind is pure and calm. It is believed that developing one's mind is the path to wisdom, which in turn leads to personal freedom and helps us maintain good conduct.

There is an Eightfold Path to follow in Buddhism, and number five of this path is Right Livelihood. This certainly indicates your work life has a definitive place in this religion. At the time it was created, *rightful* meant any occupation that did not cause unnecessary harm to other living things.

The Dalai Lama expands on the idea of right livelihood, saying that for regular people, right livelihood comes from abandoning the five wrong livelihoods—hinting, flattery, bribery, coercion, and hypocrisy—and procuring requisites truthfully, honestly, and in a non-harmful way. He says we cannot overcharge customers and clients, or exploit others. He believes we should engage in work contributing to the healthy functioning of society, and the welfare of others. He goes on to say that right livelihood is also a lifestyle free from the extremes of asceticism and luxury.

His words about avoiding "hinting, flattery, bribery, coercion, and hypocrisy" remind me of the kind of marketing we all dislike. Don't you just hate it when you feel coerced to join now before time runs out? Or, the hypocrisy of ads proclaiming the quality of something only to read the details and find a total mismatch? How about when you are falsely flattered by someone who wants your sale? These approaches are why marketing has a bad name. There's also a nugget in here about pricing. He's explicit about not overcharging clients or exploiting others. This can certainly inform our actions in setting our pricing to be of value, and to pay our vendors fairly.

I like the deeper instruction the Dalai Lama gives to look for work that contributes to the well-being of the world. But I am especially struck by his mandate, that we live not in asceticism, which is severe self-discipline and avoidance of all forms of indulgence and luxury, but rather, in the middle. I know too many purpose-driven entrepreneurs who feel bad about earning money or guilty about pursuing money. So, here we have a clear instruction on the right place to aim—in the center. This can mean you can have enough for yourself, and enough to help others.

Vietnamese Zen teacher, Thich Nhat Hanh wrote, "To practice Right Livelihood (Samyang java), you have to find a way to earn your living without transgressing your ideals of love and compassion. The way you support yourself can be an expression of your deepest self, or it can be a source of suffering for you and others." He has expanded the teaching on ethical conduct this way:

> *Aware that great violence and injustice have been done to our environment and society, we are committed not to live with a vocation that is harmful to humans and nature. We will do our best to select a livelihood that helps realize our ideal of understanding and compassion. Aware of global economic, political, and social realities, we will behave responsibly as consumers and as citizens, not supporting companies that deprive others of their chance to live.*

Most purpose-driven entrepreneurs—with their passion to make the world better in some way—have businesses that could fall under this idea of right livelihood. What could be a better way to express your deepest self than to offer your gifts to others through your business? Getting that business up and running to support you and your community is surely a divine practice.

Christianity

Christianity is the world's largest religion with approximately 2.4 billion adherents. But, Christians are a diverse group. About half are Catholic. Protestants, broadly defined as historical, Anglican, or independent, are a little over one-third. Orthodox Christians come in at 12 percent. And, other Christians, such as Mormons and Jehovah's Witnesses, make up the remaining one percent of the global Christian population. Each of these believes something different.

Which is only to say I could never come up with one concise way of sharing how Christianity advises us on our marketing. I come at this from the perspective of being a Catholic who converted to my religion later in life. This makes my point of view different from non-Catholic Christians, as well as those who were raised in the Catholic faith. The best I can do here is to try to focus on beliefs common to most Christians. If you don't feel your version of Christianity is reflected here, or are just curious about other Christian viewpoints on business, there are plenty of places to look. Start with Google, then dive into the various articles and books, until you find the version that most resonates with you.

Generally, Christians believe God is the creator of the universe and life itself. That man and woman kind were created in his image. And, that he did all of this for nothing but his glory, and the happiness of his creatures. I believe this is good news for those of us who have created a business.

When you build a successful business for the happiness of yourself, those you serve, and the community you are part of, you are stepping into the role God created for you—to live in his image. When you invent services and products that serve the world you are imitating, which is another way of praising, God's role as a creator. When you serve with the idea of creating accomplishment, magnificence or beauty, to contribute to the world God made, you are reflecting his glory.

This is different from what capitalism has led us to believe, which is that humanity is at the center of the business world. That human progress is what will move the world along, and ultimately, create personal freedom. The Christian point of view would reject that we are responsible as the sole agents in our business. As Christians, we are in business to glorify God and his intentions.

This isn't just our role; it was Jesus' role also. Jesus says he "must be about my Father's business" (Luke 2:49) and his nourishment "is to do the will of him who sent me and to finish his work" (John 4:34). Since most Christians believe Jesus' actions and life were a guideline of sorts as to how we should live our lives, we can relax a little. If Jesus came to do his father's work, can't we be content to do the same? Jesus' life was an amazing example of ongoing service to those around him, under the guidance of his father. I believe if you set up your business to do the same, you are working in accordance with God's will.

Christians also believe the Bible is a guide. Bible verses abound around working and stewarding that which we are given. They start in the beginning with "The Lord God took the man and put him in the Garden of Eden to work it and take care of it" (Genesis 2:15). It doesn't stop there. Look up Bible verses on work or business, and you'll see what I mean. Over and over, we are bid to take care of that which we are given, to work diligently, and to take care of those around us. How better to do that than to have a successful business? Your business can literally touch the lives of many—you, your clients, vendors, family, and community. Success means you can also donate money and services to those in need. When done ethically and in line with God's teachings, your business success is exactly in line with the Bible's teachings.

Another common belief among Christians is the belief in the power of grace. And, all denominations believe in the power of prayer. It seems to me it doesn't matter if your style of prayer is different from another's, whether you repeat the same prayer over and over, or pray only through Jesus or pray as on ongoing conversation directly with God. It matters that you do it in regard to your business and your marketing, so that you can be in grace with these endeavors. For me, it's the Catholic style of ritual prayer and consecration that fills my heart with grace. Find out what it is for you, and be brave enough to do it.

I'll leave this section with the scripture of 1 Peter 4, which asks us to live according to God, rather than human standards. To love each other, and offer each other hospitality—yes, even in our businesses. That "each of you should use whatever gift you have received to serve others, as faithful stewards of God's grace in its various forms." So, step into marketing the gifts you've been graced with so that others may receive them.

Confucianism

"Instead of being concerned that you are not known, seek to be worthy of being known" is a quote from Confucius I particularly like for our marketing adventure. Isn't that a wonderful sentiment? If all my clients came to me asking how to increase their worthiness of being known, I'd think I was living heaven on earth for sure. What a powerful way to ask for visibility via the capacity to serve.

Sometimes viewed as a philosophy, by others as a religion, Confucianism is a way of life taught by Confucius (Kong Fuzi) in China in the 6th-5th century BCE. He was a teacher and philosopher whose rituals and traditions shaped Chinese social relationships and moral thought. Confucianism revolves around the pursuit of the unity—to create harmony on earth, among all people. All who studied and practiced this philosophy aimed at harmonious relationships, believing it would result in greater peace in their countries. Confucians do not believe in, seek consolation from, or pray to gods. Instead, they believe people need to be grounded in the present. The attention of Confucius was solely focused on practical considerations of this world, and on everyday concerns. He was seeking a solution for the challenges of his time, a way to cure a society that was rife with political strife. Confucius said heaven was beyond our understanding so instead, we should concentrate on doing the right thing in this life. He did not provide many rules, rather, he taught a respectful attitude toward others. He encouraged his students to honor others' cultural beliefs, and to learn from every person they met.

This is striking to me because I work with purpose-driven entrepreneurs who, although want to enact change here in the physical world, often spend a lot of time contemplating the spiritual. While I think this is important—obviously, this whole book is about that on some level—I cannot emphasize enough, how important acting in the physical world is. Praying and seeking consolation from heaven is not remotely enough to have a thriving business, though I see lots of people hoping it's so in the spiritually oriented entrepreneur communities. If you instead concern yourself with taking practical steps in this world, scary though they may be, while maintaining an attitude of faith, you're enacting the divine formula of heaven on earth.

Confucius maintained that his philosophy and teachings spring from a single principle called shù, which is akin to the

English word *empathy*. From this came the original version of the Golden Rule: "What you don't want done to yourself, don't do to others" (Analects 15:24). Though Confuscism could be summed up with this single encompassing principle of empathy, there are several important virtues within this one Confucian practice I think are informative for our marketing.

The first of these is rén, which can be described as benevolence, humane, and being human. It includes a sense of dignity for all living things and humans. Rén is about mercy, love, and humanity. Confucius focused on individual development, which to him, happened within the context of human relationships. People who practice rén are motivated by a deep empathy for others, and show this with their care and humane attitude. Confucius also defined rén as: "wishing to be established himself, seeks also to establish others; wishing to be enlarged himself, he seeks also to enlarge others."

This is the perfect way to describe authentic marketing. If you can be so moved by wanting to support another—and hold that as equal to your desire to grow yourself—telling others about your business becomes easy. It's when one of these gets skewed that marketing gets hard. If you slide to the side of wanting to serve others, but not holding your own growth as equal, you'll avoid your marketing efforts. If you slide to the other side and make it all about your business' growth, you can come off as aggressive or pushy in your marketing.

The second virtue, lǐ, can be translated as rite or reason, but as it relates to social behavior, it can be termed *customs* or *rules*. Lǐ is the means for life to be ritualized and made sacred. In this way, society can be properly ordered and harmony is established. Confucius saw it as embodying all things between humanity and nature, a sort of natural law. Its Confucian meaning ranges from politeness and etiquette to proper practices to governance, with the emphasis on performance.

Lǐ can inform people about their duties to others, and of the expectations society has of them.

It's not quite like a law, though, as we might see here in the west. Rather than the kind of law that punishes after an illegal action, which makes it an external authority, Confucius argues for a ritual system connecting patterns of internalized behavior that exert influence before actions are taken. In this way, people behave properly because they believe they should, and to avoid shame or losing face.

I'm not a fan of a lot of rules and shoulds when it comes to our businesses, but I do see the value in knowing best practices, especially in marketing. Too many entrepreneurs follow their own beliefs, despite massive evidence to the contrary. There is a lot of dreaming that clients will just magically appear, people will understand your message right away, and you can avoid doing things you don't care for and still thrive. When deciding on the kind of marketing you need to do for your business, take the time to understand what experts or people who've had success suggest, or research to find suggestions for best practices. If repeatedly you find there is marketing advice for your situation that you don't like, you can't just avoid it. Rather, consider doing the inner work you may need to do on your resistance to the suggested path. In my experience, seven out of 10 times, our own issues are in the way of following practical marketing advice. Those other three times? That's truly not the path for you at this time. Knowing that and making the decision consciously makes all the difference. Then, if you should decide to go a different way, so be it, but you won't be scratching your head in bewilderment if it doesn't turn out the way you hoped.

Yì is a third important concept under this umbrella of empathy in Confucianism. Literally meaning justice or righteousness, it involves a desire to do good, and to do so with skill. Yì brings together the Confucian orientation towards cultivating benevolence, rén, and skillful practice, lǐ. It strives to find a balanced understanding, along with the insights necessary, to apply the Confucian virtues appropriately to the situation.

So, too, could be our goal with marketing. You aren't on a path to know everything about marketing, or even the right thing. You are looking for a balance of skill building, gaining insight, and having the insight to apply it appropriately. What a description of grace in action!

We'll leave this discussion of Confucianism with another great quote by Confucius: "When it is obvious that the goals cannot be reached, don't adjust the goals, adjust the action steps." This may be the best marketing advice I've ever heard! If all entrepreneurs could become fluid in this way and adjust their steps as needed, we'd have a lot more business success.

Hinduism

Hinduism is considered a way of life with guidelines on what you should and shouldn't do. Unlike Christianity or Islam, there is no founder, no one book as its basis, and no central authority or institution managing it. It adapts and changes as the practices and traditions of the times add to it. Its adherents, Hindis—who number about 1.5 billion—call it dharma, or a way to live. In the West, we call it a religion, because that's the closest word we have to describe it.

There are some core beliefs in Hinduism that can support your marketing journey. First, devout Hindis have no separation between their faith and lifestyle. In some sense, the goal of Hinduism is to understand the will God has for you, and to follow it to the best of your abilities. You can lead your everyday life, but God will be central to it and in your thoughts, always. Your profession can be as direct of a path to God as worshiping in temple. This is called karma yoga. Of course, you cannot take sole credit for your accomplishments as all belongs to God. By doing your duty to the best of your ability, you can take care of yourself, your family, and your community. If you are on the correct path, you will be met with universal support every step of the way.

This is exactly what I see so many purpose-driven entrepreneurs longing for. To have the right relationship with their spiritual nature, their business, and those around them. Hinduism offers a path for this—make God central to your thoughts and actions. Strive to figure out the plan God has for your business, and fulfill it to the best of your ability. Of course, this means marketing it well. Believing God will meet you halfway—and send support if you need it—could put many entrepreneurs' fears to rest.

Gandhi, one of the most famous peacemakers known, was born Hindi. Though he studied many religions in his adult life, he believed all his life he was faithful to Hindu tenets. He could do this because Hinduism is inclusive, tolerating all other religions, and encouraging everyone to worship God according to their own faith. Although most focus on how Gandhi's spirituality shaped his political views, I want to point out two personal traits of Gandhi's that can help in your marketing.

Gandhi was very much aware of his own personal fears, but through acknowledging them and working with their presence in his life, he managed to transform them. He realized fear would lead him to all the wrong places, so he worked constructively with this negative energy to minimize its influence on his life and his work. From a Hindi perspective, fear is a product of our ego; we are all able to work on ourselves to become more courageous. True to this sentiment, Gandhi believed courage is something that can be cultivated and developed by us all. He said, "There would be no one to frighten you if you refused to be afraid."

Fear is the number one reason I see talented, giving entrepreneurs avoid acting, distracting themselves and otherwise sabotaging their marketing efforts. Is growing your business scary? Of course! Is stepping into greater visibility unnerving? Totally. You can develop courage and lessen your fears. I like to remind my clients being brave does not mean you aren't scared—it means being scared and moving forward anyway.

Gandhi was a continual learner, and believed that evolution of ideas, thoughts, and principles was natural. This is another tenet of Hinduism—all things in the universe evolve, and this is a transformation from a beginning state to a manifested state of consciousness. You can see this in Gandhi's lifetime as he evolved his interpretation of his principles. Because of this, many inconsistencies can be found in his writings, though he readily admitted this.

> *I would like to say to the diligent reader of my writings and to others who are interested in them that I am not at all concerned with appearing to be consistent. In my search after Truth, I have discarded many ideas and learnt many news things.... What I am concerned with is my readiness to obey the call of Truth, my God, from moment to moment, and therefore, when anybody finds any inconsistency between any two writings of mine, if he still has any faith in my sanity, he would do well to choose the later of the two on the same subject.*

Imagine the relief you could feel if you held your work with the same loose grip. Not worried about how the work or writings or speech or video or social media post you did today would look in the future. You, too, are in process, and you are evolving, just like everything else in the cosmos. So, where you and your business are today is good, and where you are going is even better.

Islam

Islam is the name of a monotheistic religion whose adherents are called Muslims. Islam started in the 7th century when Muhammad began receiving divine revelations that would later form the Qur'an, the central Islam text. Muslims believe Muhammad was sent by God, whom they call Allah, to confirm the monotheistic teachings of earlier prophets like Jesus, Moses, and Abraham. The three major parts of Islam are the beliefs, ritualistic practices, and the effort to improve oneself.

Muslim people make up a majority in 50 countries and a minority in many more, and there are two divisions within the tradition—the Sunni and Shi'a. As a result, the customs and interpretations of being Muslim are colored by the history and culture the followers are part of. So, like many other religions, finding common beliefs is not straightforward.

Many Muslims practice what are called the Five Pillars, which include ongoing professing of their faith, practicing five daily prayers, making annual donations to charity, fasting during daylight hours during Ramadan, and making a pilgrimage to Mecca, a holy city in Islam where Muhammad was born, at least once in their life. And they live by laws called Shariah, that govern all aspects of their lives, including food and clothing. Clearly, Islam is a way of life, not just a religion. Here are some of the practices or beliefs I think can inform marketing.

Praying five times per day is an obligation in Islam, called Salah. Each prayer includes a series of movements and recitations from the Quran. Muslims consider prayer to be both spiritual and physical, with various standing, bending, and prostrating postures, symbolizing devotion to God. Though each prayer can be done in little time, maybe even five minutes, it is a way of totally submitting to the will of Allah, and showing your love and gratitude for him. It is a reminder throughout every day your relationship with Allah is at the center of your life. It's also a chance to reflect. Are you living in a righteous way that is pleasing to Allah? Muslims believe strongly in judgment after death, so this is a safeguard to help one live a life leading to favorable judgment in the afterlife. Although the prayers can be done anywhere, alone or with others, on Fridays, it is required for Muslims to pray together in groups at their mosque. This is to create congregation and to foster good relationships among families and communities.

Marketing, too, is a series of postures and actions that must be taken daily. You might sit down to write copy for your grand opening, stand at a networking meeting sharing with someone about the work you do, pick up your phone to follow up with three potential clients, and pencil out costs for an estimate for new work—all in the same day. If you could move through these various tasks with an idea that you are being of service to others and pleasing God, Goddess or whatever you believe is around us, you could view your day as divine. Way better than our typical day of dreading these activities.

Another major tenet of Islam is hospitality. Mona Siddiqui discusses this in her book, *Hospitality in Islam: Welcoming in God's Name*. Based in part on the story of Abraham sharing with angels, that inspired a sense of hospitality among Islam, Judaism, and Christianity, which all share Abraham as a founding person in their religions, Siddiqui says hospitality goes even deeper in Islam. She points out that the Bedouin society that preceded Islam already placed hospitality as central to a honorable character, and fundamental to the harsh desert environment where everyone receiving food and drink in a timely way, meant the difference between life or death. Besides hospitality being an honorable, charitable way of life, Siddiqui explains all the commandments are to share food and blessings with others, to give to charity, and to look after others are "because this is how God is and God's giving knows no limits."

Charitable acts then, including hospitality, are a way a Muslim can receive favor with Allah. They are also a way to create relationships beyond one's family or friends. This is not only about growing the number of those you associate with. Siddiqui makes the point that what we eat and whom we eat with has the theological significance of connecting an ordinary life with a higher one. There are also limits on hospitality, as it is a time and resource demanding act. In this way, both the receiver and the giver of hospitality must know the rules of a successful interaction. Be a good host, but also be a good guest.

Many purpose-driven entrepreneurs could benefit from this idea of being hospitable within their marketing. Content marketing is based on this very idea. Give away your best information for free, and be abundant in sharing your resources and in this way, build a loyal following of clients. Too many entrepreneurs focus on getting paid for their expertise up front, and hoard their resources for fear of being stolen from. If you can instead, find a way to share abundantly in a way that also honors your own needs for financial sustenance, you are in a good place indeed. Cause marketing is another piece springing from this hospitable attitude. If you are making good money from your endeavors but not sharing it with causes that make the world a better place, you're missing a huge opportunity for contribution and fulfillment.

Indigenous

The United Nations estimates that there are over 370 million indigenous people living in 70 countries worldwide. They are defined as people practicing unique traditions and retaining social, cultural, economic, and political characteristics distinct from those of the dominant societies in which they live. Spread across the world from the Arctic to the South Pacific, they are the descendants—according to a common definition—of those who inhabited a country or a geographical region at the time when people of different cultures or ethnic origins arrived. They are approximately 5% of our population and spread throughout hundreds of different groups. Which makes it near to impossible to find a coherent point of view to share with you here.

I'm including this category because it points out something I believe is important in a discussion such as this. The world is a diverse place. Every single one of these groups has its own spiritual approach. Just because we ended up with 12 classic religions doesn't mean that's all the resources we have. Each one of us is a descendant of a long line of people. Going back through your own lineage is a valid approach to informing yourself of the spirituality running through your genes. Or to uncover any spiritual conflicts you may be carrying if you, by chance, are a descendant of two spiritual traditions or cultures that clashed. Imagine if your ancestors were both British and Native American for example. Or Jewish and Muslim. This means that energetically you may have conflicting spiritual approaches in your gene set. Can you see how that could cause some internal conflicts about how you are in the world? Making peace with these differences may be required or you may find yourself wanting to choose one approach over another.

I'm not trying to oversimplify here. My point is that you have some conscious choice about how to proceed; looking to your original tribes approach may help you do that. I'm also pointing out we have a plethora of information to pull from when trying to construct our own spiritual approach to our business. Investigating various indigenous points of view could be helpful in creating a narrative that fits your life.

Jainism

Jainism is a religion from India in the 6th-century BCE. The creator of Jainism, Mahavira, lived in the same time and age as Buddha, Confucius, and Lao-tzu. Jainism was a reaction to Hinduism, which was caste based. Early on, Jainism accepted people of all castes. Rather than the middle way that Buddha saw between good and evil, Mahavira believed good was contained in the soul as life and covered by matter from the material world which was non-life and contained evil. The goal of life is to liberate the soul from its material confines.

The essence of Jainism is nonviolence (ahimsa). This is, in part, because Jains believe the whole universe is alive and therefore, has a soul. It is considered that each of these souls is equal, and should be treated with compassion and respect. Jains are strict vegetarians and minimize their use of resources. They don't take jobs harming animals and may even sweep the path before them, as they walk in order not to step on insects. It's also because the aim of Jainism is to eliminate all karma from the soul to achieve liberation. By avoiding violence of any kind, they believe it is less likely to add new karma to their soul (jiva). To help reduce the karma they have accrued, they follow a disciplined life path of avoiding indulgences and material goods, along with moral cultivation.

The cultivation Jainism requires is to follow the core practice of the three jewels. These jewels are right belief, right knowledge, and right conduct. If one were to vastly simplify these, you could say instead: believe in the faith, study the faith, and follow the directives of the faith. Of course, there is more to it than that.

Right belief—also called right view, right perception, or right faith—has to do with seeing the difference between good and bad, right and wrong, truth and untruth, as well as avoiding misconceptions, such as beliefs or superstitions, getting in the way of seeing clearly. You must be determined to find what is true, and distinguish it from what is untrue. This is the jewel of spiritual development, where one renounces material comforts, and begins to release doubt. It is intertwined with the remaining two jewels because without it, the other two are not possible.

You would be well served if you took this same position in your marketing. You cannot take in all the hype in the marketing world as truth. A lot of it simply isn't. Can you make six figures in 12 weeks of a new business? Not usually. How about get hundreds of new clients with no effort or money on your part? Nope. Grow your business without sweating through creating your messaging and branding? Uh-uh.

Also, not all good advice is true for *your* business. So, you need to wade through, looking for your truth. A big part of this is clearing out your own limiting beliefs and misconceptions that get in the way of seeing this truth. Another part involves living out your marketing plans with the sincere search for truth. This takes some skill building in the art of discernment—which means you begin to understand the nuances of truth that apply to you.

Take right perception, add to it understanding, and you get right knowledge. This second jewel is about having an accurate understanding of the true nature of the universe. There are eight different types of knowing in Jainism, including mental, acquired, distant, paranormal, and absolute, which are good, along with false types that include invalid knowledge, erroneous knowledge, and wrong knowledge.

How I long for us to use more ways of seeing in the marketing world. If you spend some time reading about each of these types of knowing, you begin to see we have many faculties to use in understanding a problem or deciding how to move forward. By consciously choosing a type of knowing, you can both garner the rewards from it while respecting its limitations. In other words, by knowing a lot about knowing, you can make better decisions. I see many people in the marketing world using only one type of knowing and then, wondering why their decisions don't lead to success.

Judaism

Judaism is a monotheistic religion developed among the ancient Israelites some 1500 years before Christianity. Today, it encompasses the religion, philosophy and culture of over 14 million Jewish people worldwide. Judaism has a wide collection of texts, practices, beliefs, and forms of organization, with the Torah as its foundational text.

A central practice in Jewish tradition is the observance of the Sabbath *(Shabbat)*. The Hebrew word "Shabbat" comes from the root *Shin-Beit-Tav*, meaning to cease, to end, or to rest. It is a day of complete rest and spiritual rejuvenation. But as Ana Levy-Lyons, author of *No Other Gods: The Politics of the Ten Commandments*, states: "To equate the Sabbath with an ordinary vacation is to mistake its essence and its revolutionary potential. The goal of a Sabbath practice is not to patch us up and send us back out to the world ... but to reclaim a full day every week to luxuriate in life's fountain of blessings."

Jewish theologian Abraham Joshua Heschel writes from a mystical perspective in the rabbinic tradition, describing the Sabbath as a gift from God, a "palace in time." Heschel reframed the experience of Shabbat from a day of ceasing the important work of daily life to instead live a full twenty-five hours outside of time. He said "... *the Sabbath is the counterpoint of living; the melody sustained throughout all agitations and vicissitudes which menace our conscience; our awareness of God's presence in the world.*"

Understanding Shabbat as a radical act of freedom is not only a reminder that, historically, the Jewish people had to participate in their own liberation from slavery in Egypt, it also challenges us in our modern world to find ways to free ourselves from shoulds, demands and obligations, from our salary and any other form of work. That we have the capacity to say "I'm taking a day off." And that all the cosmos supports us in this as it mirrors the very way that God created the world. To work hard for six days and enjoy the sweet bliss of just being in it on the seventh day.

Setting aside a day of rest could be the perfect practice for the owner of a small business. How often do we push, push, and push forward, always working, even though we likely chose working for ourselves as a way to have more freedom? What if you looked to the practice of Shabbat instead? How could you organize yourself and your marketing efforts in a way that pushed for completion and asked you to routinely step back to enjoy it? I'm guessing that it would not only reduce any reluctance you have in your marketing, but also bring in divine inspiration and point of view that could ensure your success.

I look to a book called *Jewish Wisdom for Business Success: Lessons for the Torah and Other Ancient Texts* to find another point that I believe is pertinent for marketing.

In this teaching, author Levi Brackman focuses on finding our inner will and bringing about our outer will to match it. According to the Torah, our inner will is already inside us, we just have to find it. The Jewish mystics, the Kabbalists, called it *"pnimiyut ha-ratzon,"* which means "inner will" or "authentic self." It's often veiled or wrapped up in what is called the *"chitzoniyut ha-ratzon"* or the "outer will." This inner will is something that expresses our authentic self. Brackman feels that we will have the most success if we can find that thing which we are most passionate about, the thing which is clearly an expression of our authentic self, figure out the commercial application for it and then, market that. This goes hand in hand with the fact that the authentic self always wants to be creative. It gives us the fundamental drive to create a reality that did not previously exist.

Many Torah scholars believe the universe was created by God's outer will, to serve a higher and inner divine desire and will. So, when we find our inner will and use it to shape our outer will, we are again enacting God's creative process. This inner will is powerful in its effect, on the motivation and passion we need, to achieve what we really want in life.

Turning inward to find your true passion is a powerful place to market from. Too many entrepreneurs set up their business around what others tell them they are good at. But if your inner will isn't in alignment with this outer talent, it won't flow well. When you can find your deepest passion, and take steps to figuring out a way to enact that in exchange for money, you've found the winning combination of a purpose driven business. When you share this inner passion, or what I call your deep why, your marketing comes across with more authenticity. Clients respond to this kind of sharing, with delight, rather than feeling they've been sold to. It's a win for you both. And if by doing this, you are enacting a divine process, all the better.

New Thought

Did you know if you believe in affirmations, metaphysics, or the law of attraction you were practicing a religious act? Neither did I. Though, honestly, I've practiced all these things at one time or another. The religion is called New Thought, and started in the United States in the 19th century. It's best understood as a loosely allied group of religious denominations, secular membership organizations, authors, philosophers, and individuals who share beliefs concerning metaphysics, positive thinking, the law of attraction, healing, life force, creative visualization, and personal power[9].

It was considered by many to have been derived from the unpublished writings of Phineas Quimby, and furthered by many who studied under him and beyond. Organizations that sprang from this movement include Divine Science, Unity Church, and Religious Science. If you didn't come across them organizationally in the 20th century, you might have read a book instead. Two of the best-selling books of all time, *Think and Grow Rich* by Napoleon Hill and *You Can Heal Your Life* by Louise Hay came from this philosophy. One of the beliefs of New Thought, the law of attraction, gained a lot of attention in 2006 from the film, *The Secret*.

Some might dismiss this religion as being trite and only concerned with positive thinking, but that would be a mistake. This tradition is 150 years old and continuing. Wasn't Christianity dismissed in its early days, too? We might conjecture that any new approach in religion would be questioned as possible heresy, but it should not stop us from considering the ideas and investigating the actual beliefs, rather than dismissing them based on media interpretation.

Working from April Moncrieff's *The Principles of New Thought*, I found these points for our discussion on how this approach might inform marketing.

First, the basis for New Thought is a metaphysical understanding of the world. This means it focuses on the world outside our objective and physical understanding. Traditional Christian teachings are seen as symbolic, rather than literal. New Thought adherents see the characters and places in the Bible as an outer representation of the conditions and states of consciousness within us. In looking at Jesus' life and experiences in the Bible, they understand it as living symbolism representing a universal human experience.

This metaphysical approach includes views of God going beyond the idea of God as a human-like, fatherly figure. It posits that God is infinite and everywhere, in all space and time. The best relationship we can have is direct and personal.

The goal of prayer is not to ask for outside help in solving this or that problem, but rather, to merge our human selves with the divine. In New Thought, there is an emphasis on this inner attunement, of quieting the conscious mind and transcending the "ceaseless torrent of thoughts, by developing the art of focusing the awareness inwardly, for impressions and guidance, from the higher Source." This higher state of consciousness is not reserved for a select few; it is a path available to all.

I've seen people be in heaven with their marketing or the other place, where it's pure torture. Dread, doubt, resistance, and outright terror rear their heads around standing up to speak in front of others or making a follow-up call. If, instead, they could quiet their emotions and attune with the divine mind, they could avoid many of these bad feelings. I doubt your creator wants you to feel sleazy while marketing your business. Maybe you could get tuned in and check.

The ability of consciousness to recreate the body and restore it to its rightful pattern as the image and likeness of God is taught, embraced, and practiced throughout the New Thought movement. On a deeper look, you can see that New Thought practitioners believe in a unity of the body, mind, and spirit as necessary for good health. Rather than the simplified version in the media that portrays as practitioners who refuse traditional medical treatments (that could cure their disease), many New Thought practitioners are busy practicing preventative medicine, taking good care of their bodies with diet, exercise and supplements and are highly involved in their medical care when there is a breakdown. They are just as likely to pray for guidance in their approach as to listen to only one voice of an MD, who ignores their spirit in his/her treatment[10].

It's the same for your marketing. You can bring your marketing efforts into alignment with it's rightful pattern of unity with your body, mind, and soul. That's healthy marketing that gets good results. Also, it's never too late. No matter how it's gone in the past, you can always step into new, better behaviors, and get better results. If you can just keep your divine mind in your business, pay close attention, and act daily, then it will happen. Most successful people you meet have a trail of failures behind them. If they can do it, so can you.

Paganism

Modern Paganism includes reconstructed historical religions in the modern world and modern blended traditions, such as Wicca and Druidism. Keep in mind that before the 20th century, Pagans would have never called themselves Pagan. This was a word used by early Christians to define someone who was not part of the Christian church. These historical religions then, are really a collection of many types of spiritualties, indigenous to a variety of places and old ways of worshipping. These were generally from Greco-Roman, Celtic, Germanic, Slavic tribes. Modern paganism is currently practiced in Europe, North America, Australia, New Zealand, and Iceland.

Because of its diversity in origins and practitioners, it's hard to say exactly what all Pagans believe. There are some themes that stand out in regards to a spiritual informing of your marketing. The first is that Pagans generally honor both God and Goddess. That means both the masculine and feminine divine sit as at least equal. There are some who believe the Goddess gets even more emphasis. I believe this kind of gender equality can be a powerful way to approach your marketing, indeed even your whole business. It means feminine ways of promoting and working are just as valid as the traditional masculine ways we've been taught to embrace. It also respects receiving intuition, taking care of others, and using transformation as fine tools in your marketing. You can nurture relationships, meander a bit, follow your hunches, and still succeed. It's not all about a straight line that you forcefully follow forward. It's also not that only one form of the Goddess is revered. Maiden, mother, and crone are all revered aspects of her nature, meaning young, free ways of being are encouraged alongside the caring, supportive mothering role, and the wisdom that comes with experience.

Gods, too, are multifaceted. From managing fertility to all of nature, Pagan Gods create, protect, and cherish. They are both old and young and strong. This is not to pit women against men, as we humans have both a feminine and masculine side. It is to recognize the power of claiming *both*. Paganism suggest to do our marketing well, we must be whole.

Paganism believes that both the God and Goddess are spiritual, sexual, and human. This gets at the total of human nature—we are not just one thing but multifaceted beings, with human connections and desires, along with erotic sides and spiritual longings. This suggests that you can be real in your marketing, and still be well received by others. Indeed, I've seen many people shy away from working with someone who seemed too perfect or too together, opting instead to work with someone who sits in their vulnerabilities, mistakes, and longings while still striving to be their best.

Paganism sees divinity as inherent in nature and humanity, and views all things as interconnected. This often creates a connection to ecology and the environment, and an interest in the natural life cycle and seasonal patterns. I would strongly suggest you take this on in your marketing: There are times to act and times to rest. Because everything is connected and nothing exists alone, then every action has a consequence. There is no concept of sin or forgiveness in Pagan ethics. The consequences of one's actions must be weighed before acting to prevent harm; if harm occurs, then reparations are made as necessary. As a result, pagans enjoy personal freedom within a framework of personal responsibility; they have few rules to follow except the main one: harm to none. This creates a focus of equitable and just ways of being in life and in business, suggesting pagans would run their business not only for profit, but also to better society, support the environment, and treat others equitably. I can think of no better recipe for a winning business for any purpose-driven entrepreneur!

Shinto

Sometimes called Japan's indigenous religion, there is no record of when exactly Shinto started or who it was founded by. I culled my knowledge of Shintoism from a third-generation practitioner, Motohisa Yamakage, in his book *The Essence of Shinto: Japan's Spiritual Heart*. Let's look at what Shinto can offer our marketing journey.

Yamakage says Shinto is a religion evolving out of the life and experience of the Japanese island people, shaped and nurtured by countless unknown men and women, over the centuries. He feels this illustrates one of the first premises of Shinto, which is that it is nature, not human beings, who teach. The Shinto religion could be defined by its reverence of nature.

Shinto believes everything comes to existence as a child-spirit of the great original spirit, Kami of the universe. Kami then, is the sustaining life energy from nature. This means humans, animals, and all natural matter, in their innermost essence, are children of this original spirit, called Naohinomitama. The meaning of ceremonies, food rituals, and prayers expresses followers' awareness that they owe their lives and sustaining life energy to Kami, the great source of nature. As they increase their awareness that they receive everything as a grace of Kami, they get a clearer perception of Naohinomitama, as the child-spirit of the great original spirit dwelling within all.

If everything is received as a grace of Kami, and we have this spirit within us, then our marketing, too, can be filled with grace. We can learn to ways of being visible more successfully from nature. My clients and I often feel better when we take a marketing question or problem with us outside. Whether it's a quick walk, a breath of fresh air, or a deep sojourn into the wild, we often find our answers with the spirit of nature close by.

With no founder, there is no system or writings connected to a founder's teachings. Though the Kojiki and the Nihonshoki chronicles have many Shinto themes, they are not sacred texts like the Bible or the Torah. In these Japanese writings, history, myths, and theology are blended with political thoughts and embellishments, and so, need to be read and interpreted with care because every word is not necessarily considered sacred. Additionally, books written by Shintoists do not attempt to set out doctrine for the whole of Shinto. No explanation then is absolute, but when we put the different explanations together, we can begin to see the essence of Shinto philosophy.

I teach marketing in this way. No memorized elevator pitches, as there are no perfect set of words. When you try to get it right in your sharing, you are cut off from the essence of the moment. Instead of being perfect or right, there is only your embodiment of your experience and your authentic effort to be what you are marketing. Then you can respond in the moment, rather than use canned, memorized stuff.

Shinto then, is a religion in which there are no absolute codes, orders, or laws. It has no founder, no doctrine, no commandments, no idols, and no organization. This sounds a lot like marketing to me, and possibly why it can feel so absolutely confusing for someone who doesn't have much experience with it. Not trying to go broad, but rather, trying to narrow it down to what works for you.

There is an underlying philosophy in Shinto of purification, which has four aspects. These can be understood by the terms clean, bright, right, and straight. The first three are about purifying and cleansing one's physical body of sins, faults, low energy vibrations, and unclean spirits. All these things get in the way of being in the physical world in a beneficial way.

The fourth—purification of the mind—means purifying our words and thoughts to think and experience reality in a straight way. This will help us not to be affected by low vibrating spirits. To do this, we must put our chaotic thoughts in order and focus on finding truth. This can come from reading inspiring spiritual books, or listening to teachers or masters who have undergone disciplined, spiritual training. It is not good enough to understand these books and lectures with only the brain, but also, with the heart. It is important to take time to examine one's own heart and mind, one's feelings and motives to cultivate cleanness and brightness. We must keep our mind firmly at the center of our body, the center of our true self, to avoid it falling out of balance.

I like the holistic approach Shinto uses to keep on the correct path. Authentic marketing, too, comes from this holistic path. Truly, it is your state of being and purity of intentions bringing about marketing outcomes. To get the results you want, you must be clear and straight in your thinking—and inspired in both brain and heart.

Even though human beings are tainted with mistakes, faults, or uncleanness in this world, they can rise to the status of Kami by showing continuous improvement and progress on their individual journey. It doesn't happen by natural growth, but rather, with spiritual training and exercises, such as misogi, along with practicing the work of love and charity to cultivate a clean and pure character. In Shinto, the process of creating and birthing life and spirit is described as musubi, and is held in very high regard. In the end, Shinto professes the belief that there is no absolute and final salvation. There's only the ability to continue growing, maybe even to grow so far as to become Kami.

So, too, is marketing a path for growth. Continuous improvement and progress is possible. In fact, when you reach for greater visibility within your business, it's demanded. To reach these new heights, you'll have to shed former limitations and fears.

Sikhism

Sikhism is the fifth largest religion in the world. It is a monotheistic religion, and was founded in the 16th century in the Punjab region of India during a time of conflict between Hinduism and Islam. It was first created as an alternative to these two religions by Guru Nanak, and developed further by the nine gurus who followed him. Sikhs regard the 10 Gurus not as divine, but as enlightened teachers through whom God revealed his will. Guru Granth Sahib is the religious scripture of Sikhism, written by the Gurus with their teachings along with some traditions and teachings of Indian saints. This scripture is regarded by Sikhs as the final and eternal living Guru, coming after the lineage of the 10 human Sikh gurus.

In Sikhism beliefs, there are three duties every Sikh must do in their lives. The first is Nam Japna, which is always keeping God in mind by repeating and focusing the mind on his name or identity. This is done by meditation, vocal singing of Shabads, hymns from the Sri Guru Granth Sahib, or the chanting of the various names of God. This act of singing, quiet meditation, and listening to sacred text or sacred words is a very important activity in the everyday life of a Sikh. The second is Kirt Karna, which is earning an honest living. This doesn't just mean avoiding crime; Sikhs avoid gambling, begging, or working in the alcohol or tobacco industries. They are supposed to carry out good deeds and earn a honest, pure, and truthful livelihood by exercising their God-given skills, abilities, talents and hard labor for the benefit and improvement of the individual, their family and society at large. And the third, Vand Chhakna, is a practice of giving to charity and caring for others.

Any one of these three practices would make your marketing stronger. Do all three and you'll be unstoppable. Chanting or praying to God or source continually keeps you in divine mind. This is a perfect state to do your marketing from. Exercising your skills and abilities in service to the world is a fulfilling way to spend your days. And giving to charity through your work is a strong component of authentic marketing.

Now, let's turn to the work of Dr. Upinder Jit Kaur in her paper *The Role and Status of Women in Sikhism* to understand how the Sikh concepts of equality, married life, and women can influence your marketing approach.

Sikhism believes God is gender neutral, and seeks to transcend ideas of caste, creed, clime, sex, and color. The Sikh Gurus strove to create an egalitarian and progressive society. They advocated principles of universal equality and humanity for all. The founding Sikh Gurus even held the woman equal to man in all respects. They pleaded for equal rights and privileges for her, both in religious and socio-political fields, they also placed women in positions of power within their community. They even let them fight in wars. This started in the 15th century, roughly 350 years before the women's emancipation movement in Europe. In an age when the inferiority of women was given, the Guru insisted women must be treated with respect as her mothering is the source of man's very existence and the entire life of society.

Feeling a sense of equality is a powerful platform from which to market. Too often, entrepreneurs feel not as good as others they perceive to be more successful, more talented or luckier than they are. This less-than feeling keeps them thinking small, or that they don't have what it takes. So, too, their marketing has a small voice and is done in a way that doesn't convey confidence.

Beyond equality, Dr. Kaur explains a Sikh is ordained to be an "ascetic within and secular without." They are asked to conduct themselves in the worldly surroundings with a spiritual inside. Dr. Kaur notes the householder's life—what we would call family life—is an essential element of social life and social structure in the Sikh religion. By combining these two, a Sikh shares in the riches of life, but never loses sight of the highest reality of the divine.

This idea of creating and well managing a household is foundational in Sikhism. They believe it is a means by which the souls grow spiritually. In Sikhism, spiritual freedom does not come from suppressing human desires but instead, by engaging in them moderately. It downplays uncontrolled appetites, and looks to households as a practical way for taming and controlling the biological instincts. Self-restraint and self-control are stressed, over and over in Sikh scripture. Besides creating growth for the people in them, Sikhism believes healthy households helps people to fulfill their obligations to society more effectively.

I like this practical approach for your marketing. It calls for a careful organization of your personal life in a way that supports you in marketing your business. Whatever household may mean to you, it's important to manage it well, and grow within it. So often we are stressed out at home and that spills into our office or networking event where we are expecting ourselves to be on and perfect. Why not instead, just be a human, set in a community, and creating partnerships supporting our growth to spiritual achievement, both personally and professionally?

Spiritual But Not Religious

According to a study conducted by Pew Research Center, one fifth of the U.S. public and one third of adults under the age of 30 are reportedly unaffiliated with any religion; however, they identify as being spiritual in some way. Of these religiously unaffiliated Americans, 37% classify themselves as spiritual but not religious, while 68% say they do believe in God, and 58% feel a deep connection to the Earth[11].

Given the lack of belief in the traditional, you might expect this group called Spiritual But Not Religious (SBNR) to be made of so many differing beliefs that no coherence could be found. Linda Mercadante, who interviewed hundreds of these people for her book *Belief without Borders,* has instead, found startling similarities. While it's not a formal religion, the spiritual approach of this group can offer some insights on approaching our marketing. Let's take a look.

Laughing at her chapter nine subtitle, *A Mobile Home In The Spiritual Universe,* I nevertheless found it descriptively accurate. What could better explain attitudes like wanting a morality that realistically responds to our diverse, changing culture and brings with it tolerance and harmony among people? Tired of religious conflict, SBNRs want compassion and peace to sit alongside individual rights, personal responsibility, and self-determination. They long for us all to find the sacred in the ordinary, even that "they are calling us back to the awe and mystery we should feel in the face of God." They insist caring for the planet is necessary. They are also open to scientific discoveries about consciousness. It's hard to imagine a more "distinctly American brand of spirituality" as Mercadante describes them.

One of the main common beliefs of this group is what Mercadante calls a shift in authority. This is "moving authority, trust, belief and divinity itself from 'out there' to 'in here,'" essentially moving the spiritual authority from God, or the church, to oneself. She maintains that it is possibly not the death of God but rather a shift in where spiritual instinct resides. They believe that everyone has the freedom to decide their own beliefs and practices with teachers or group practices as optional. It's up to each person's own inner voice to find spirituality and enlightenment.

It's hard to conjure up a better fit for an entrepreneur, especially those who left corporate life to hang their own shingle. Of course, you can do this while maintaining any religious affiliation, but if you're not part of an organized way of worshipping, take heart. You aren't alone, and here's a model for making the move to market yourself—shift your center of authority from corporate to personal.

Corporate forms of marketing rarely work for the solopreneur or tiny entrepreneur business. You must find the styles of marketing that work best for a micro business. Toss out the advice you see in Forbes or Entrepreneur magazine; they are meant for much larger companies. You now have the role of sorting through all the marketing options available to you, and determining what is best for your unique business. Yes, you can find teachers or experts to give you advice, but in the end, it's up to you to find the right mix for the person you are and the business you are trying to create, which is as unique as your fingerprints.

In general, most SBNRs find religions constricting, confining, and/or unethical. Since they don't believe religions are necessary for spiritual development, most wonder why they should deal with groups who don't meet their expectations, or behave in ways they don't always agree with. From their point of view, all religions are essentially the same, meaning they are different views of the one truth. If that's the case, why not choose what works for them from each and leave what doesn't?

I am reminded of many purpose-driven entrepreneurs, who feel such a distaste for what's happening in the business world today. Tired of unethical behavior and unsavory marketing tactics, they have a real longing for what is authentic and caring in our business lives. But take heed: Mercadante found that many SBNRs never found the place they were craving for within their spirituality. From my perspective, it's because they get stuck in the judging. In your own business, you cannot spend a lot of time in distaste for the business world and expect prosperity to descend. You can, however, use your unease for something to propel you toward a path that *does* work for you. By digesting what's not working and consciously working through it, you can create something new. Look at what you *don't* like in these business practices, and create a way you *do* like that feeds your soul. Prosperity and peace will follow.

SBNR's see God as a divine consciousness or energy that is all around us, and, in fact, in everything. This means there are no distinctions between our world and the spiritual. It's all one. We are God, too. But many take it even further. They see the divine as not independently conscious, but rather, that our experience gives experience to this consciousness. In other words, our growth helps the divine consciousness grow.

Good thing because overwhelmingly, the SBNR crowd's "primary spiritual commitment was to themselves and their own growth." They are mostly sure that well-being, comfort, and happiness are the standard measures for human achievement and assessing human action. If this, in turn, feeds the divine consciousness, it's a win-win. For many, this growth has helped them find the inner peace, happiness, self-knowledge, and stress reduction they were not able to find elsewhere. Living in a world that seems to border on chaos and be overwhelming, SBNRs look to their inner experience, rather than looking outward to society-based standards.

A parallel I see to marketing here is that this approach must begin with *you*. As much as you may want to serve others, you can best do so by being well-seated within yourself. This is the airplane adage to put on your own mask before assisting others. In my experience, the entrepreneurial journey pushes your buttons. This means that as you move your business along, personal issues will arise. This offers you the chance to clear out old limitations and beliefs making you feel less than who you really are. In this way, you are contributing not only to your own growth, but to the growth of divine consciousness. It doesn't have to stop here. As your own well-being grows, you are more and more in the position to give to others.

Finally, SBNRs tend to see human nature as inherently good. This may be a reaction against Western religious view of original sin and fallen man. Most were hard pressed to believe humans were evil or even bad, preferring to believe that people make choices that serve their evolution—or don't. They have a strong sentiment to live and let live, though they hope people will exercise their inherent nature oriented toward good for themselves and others. SBNRs often used psychological explanations such as poor parenting, deprivations, or the environment people finds themselves in for pushing them to do bad things, even while believing free choice could help them make better or worse choices.

I especially see this playing out with my clients who have experienced stress, trauma, or abuse. Too often, entrepreneurs are not seated in their own sense of goodness. In fact, they are pretty sure there is something wrong with or bad about them specifically. This perspective offers another viewpoint. What if you *are* inherently good? What if circumstances you found yourself in—stressful or dysfunctional environment, unskilled parents, abusive people—were responsible for shaping some of your reactions and actions in the world? It's possible that you can now choose differently. Healing and embracing your goodness and all that it entails, such as success and contribution, may be possible not only by grace, but by your own actions.

Taoism

In stark contrast to the active-on-your-own-behalf approach of the Spiritual But Not Religious, the concept of non-action (wu wei) is foundational to Taoism. This may be a difficult concept for us to grasp here in the West. Wu wei tells us the correct way to act is precisely *not* to act. That doesn't mean not doing or acting only in moderation, but rather, not forcing the situation or finding effortless action. To practice wu-wei is to orient with the Tao, so much so, your actions are hardly noticeable.

Taoist philosophy suggests the universe works when left to its own ways. When people exert their will against the world in a manner out of rhythm with the cycles that exist, they may disrupt the harmony. As a result, unintended consequences may develop rather than the goal they were striving for. However, Taoism does not identify people's will as the root problem. Rather, it asserts they must place their will in harmony with the natural universe. Thus, a potentially harmful interference may be avoided, and on the wings of grace, goals can be achieved effortlessly.

This reminds me of some of my more spiritual colleagues. It's common in my circles to hear them say they've delayed this or that project because it didn't feel right or didn't seem to be the right timing. Often, this decision turns out to be correct, and the project comes about in a better way at another time, or is replaced by something else ultimately a better fit for the entrepreneur or the business. Or, they regret not listening to their inner knowing when the client they had a hunch not to work with turns out to be a bad fit. Tuning in and acting on what you sense between your business and the unseen world is a powerful way to make business decisions.

It needs to go both ways. To be successful, people also need to act when they get the green light (and not just listen to the don't or delay energies). The unsuccessful ones often start questioning whether the green-light guidance is accurate at that moment, and they let anxiety and worry overshadow their capacity to move forward. Although it can be unnerving in modern day society to follow this path, I believe this concept of wu-wei can serve you well if you allow it. When you link up with the universal cycles and harmony that exist, you are giving your business a powerful ally.

Taoism is a religious tradition of Chinese origin from the 4th century BCE. Lao-tzu is purported as the author of the *Tao Te Ching,* which is considered the cornerstone text for Taoism. It's unclear whether he lived as a contemporary to Confucius in the 6th century BCE, or 200 years before that in the 4th century—or existed at all. Some scholars think the *Tao Te Ching* was compiled by a number of Taoist monks. Unlike Confucius, who sought harmony in the ordering of social life through rigidly defined ritual, Lao-tzu's philosophy looked to nature as life's ultimate guide and put the focus on the individual, rather than the societal.

Taoism holds that the goal of life is for each person to find their own harmonious alignment with the rhythm of the natural world, and to follow the Way, or the Tao, of the universe. It is based on the observation of the patterns of change in nature happening outside of us in the physical world, as well as inside of us. It emphasizes a theme of naturalness, which is considered primal to being human. If you can come into alignment with the elemental patterns of change, you will find spontaneous and creative ways to be with your actions that produce health and happiness. This demands freeing yourself from desire and selfish interest, and learning to appreciate simplicity.

We've all seen people who seem to get this natural way of living. They seem to spontaneously follow the correct path bringing them success and happiness. We all want that; so, isn't it nice to think there might be a way open to each of us to find it? And, that it's not just for a special few, but available to all who seek it? When we quiet our inner desires and observe the patterns of change in and around us, we find a guidance system for making our way. It's not complicated, but rather, comes through focusing on the simple. Though, I'm not saying it's always easy! Simple guidance sounds pretty good to me when it comes to marketing. By tuning both inward and out, and setting aside complicated, and often contradictory desires (I want to make tons of money AND only work when I feel like it) we are left with simple, where we might find our spontaneity and creativity to support us in our marketing path.

Taoism can be thought of as a path of spiritual cultivation. Besides following the Way, there are three treasures one should cultivate. The first is about having the capacity to empathize with others. It is compassion springing from the understanding that all things are interconnected. This can be described as compassion, tenderness, mercy, kindness, or benevolence. The second could be translated as frugality, moderation, restraint, or simplicity of desire. To be sparing and not excessively pursuing material wealth, stature or prestige will lead to a joyful life. The economy of nature does not waste anything.

The third, *Bugan wei tianxia xian,* translated as "not dare to be first/ahead in the world," could be translated as humility or modesty. This can either be a way of loving life or avoiding early death. To be out in front, pushing beyond where others are is a vulnerable position that can expose you to destructive forces in the world, while remaining behind gives you time to fully ripen and bear fruit. This is the humility to help or set an example from behind the scenes. Lao-tzu says this quality is especially important in leadership. Good leaders are those that people barely know exist. When good leaders' work is done, their people will say that they did it themselves.

Good marketing feels similar. When done well, customers will feel they made their decision based on their own desire, never experiencing buyers' remorse. It's easy to put yourself out there and market your services when you approach it with a simplicity and modesty. Wanting to serve with humility and to bear fruit for your clients, is attractive indeed.

Zoroastrianism

Zoroastrianism may be the world's oldest monotheistic religion. This religion was one of the most powerful religions for 1,000 years when it was the state religion of the pre-Islamic Persian empires, from 600 BCE until 650 CE. After it was suppressed and reduced in size by a Muslim conquest, and because it does not take converts—rather, one must be born into the religion—it is now one of the smallest religions with fewer than 200,000 adherents.

It was founded from the visions of the Persian prophet, Zarathustra, who was later called Zoroaster by the Greeks. It is thought that Ahura Mazda (Wise God) appeared to the prophet, Zoroaster, in the form of a vision that revealed to him secrets about creation, and gave him instructions for humanity. It is believed the teachings given to Zoroaster are in the Avesta, the sacred book of Zoroastrianism.

The beliefs in Zoroastrianism may sound familiar. It's possible this religion influenced the later-founded religions of Judaism, Islam, and Christianity. Concepts that originated in Zoroastrianism include: monotheism, prayer, the cosmic struggle between good and evil, heaven/ hell, celestial angels and archangels mediating between God and humanity, free will, judgment after death, the coming of a Messiah at the end of creation, and an apocalypse ending in the final triumph of good.

The Zoroastrian believes the world has two forces: good and evil. Arrogance, injustice, and fear represent evil while truth, honesty, justice, and purity represent good. All humans are asked to choose between these forces, either following the laws and teachings of God, or following the evil ways of the world. At the end of life, they will be judged by their choices. Ahura Mazda provided people with the knowledge of how to live a good life, and how to cleanse sin. But, in the end, those who have sinned will face the consequences of their actions.

Marketing is similar— choices we must make, over and over. It's a rare business owner who doesn't need to keep making marketing decisions. What to do, how to get started, how to do it again, or whether it needs to be adjusted. On and on, the process goes, and in the end, our results are an outcome of those choices.

The basic principle of Zoroastrianism is expressed in the phrase "good thoughts, good words, good deeds" which are humata, hukhta and huveshta, respectively. In this way, a person with their actions, rather than their fate, can bring the divine to the physical plane. This phrase serves as a practical guide for day-to-day living. Whatever the task—from drinking wine and eating food to working and spending time with the family, the guiding principle is always whether such acts are impairing someone's ability to think good thoughts, speak good words, and do good actions.

So, too, in marketing, this focus can serve you. The next time you are writing copy, or planning a campaign, consider whether you are doing it from a place of good thoughts, good words and good actions. Don't let doubt or dread guide your activities. Likewise, don't exaggerate or act arrogantly. Come from goodness, and you will create the same.

Fire plays a big role in the rituals of Zoroastrianism. Fire is a source of light, and light represents wisdom, while darkness represents ignorance. The temporal fire is the fire of creation. Not only is it considered one of the sacred elements making life possible through creation and the home hearth flame, it is also the spiritual fire within us that illuminates the path of asha, or righteous living. The spiritual fire will be diminished with bad or negative thoughts; so, it's important that the spiritual fire is kept free from anything that will dampen the flame.

Of course, I believe you are more effective in your marketing when you keep your spiritual fires burning. You may not share the same beliefs that fuel the Zoroastrian, but this concept will support you if you tend to your spirit and nurture it. When you allow order and honesty to dominate your thoughts, your marketing efforts will reflect that with authenticity and effectiveness.

ACKNOWLEDGEMENTS

My deepest gratitude to my developmental editor, Lynda McDaniels. Thank you for shaping my ramblings and offering your unwavering optimism that there was something here. Your work helped me believe this could really happen. Tina Morlock, thank you for making my final line edits in such a speedy way. Yael, sending boundless gratitude and love to you for the many ways you touch my life. Your continual sharing of your spiritual knowledge nourishes me and my whole family. Thank you to my lovely colleagues in my business strategy circle: Cynthia, Victoria, Lisa, Susan, Trisha and Lorilee for your patient support each month. To my amazing clients who impress and inspire me weekly. You keep me growing and humble me with your courage. Thank you for letting me share your stories. My dear community and friends, thank you for patiently inquiring how my book was going and listening to me about it for these years. Santiago, mi vida, I cannot put into words how much your ongoing support and acceptance means to me and my journey. I love you. For my intelligent, warm, and humorous children—you are my greatest joy and source of growth. And finally, thank you to Sonoma County for being this special place to live. The beauty and abundance around me is a source of replenishment for my soul.

ABOUT THE AUTHOR

Meet Linda—a transformational leadership coach with a marketing background—that supports entrepreneurs in growing their businesses, their impact and their revenue. Bringing together business and spirituality, Linda inspires clients to change expectations and perceptions, and step into profound personal power and excel in business. Her warm and engaging approach show just how powerful connection and simply being human in our marketing can be.

For 23 years Linda was in the visual design and marketing industry, where she created brands and campaigns for companies like Kimpton Hotels & Restaurants, Domaine Chandon, Jamba Juice, Disney, Coldwell Banker, Xerox, and many small businesses. She's received a Silver ADDY award for her brand work and has helped her clients win many awards and placements in publications such as The Wall Street Journal, TIME Magazine, and the front cover of WIRED magazine.

Linda holds degrees in graphic arts and leadership. She happily resides in Sonoma County with her husband and children.

JOIN THE RELUCTANT MARKETER COMMUNITY

Now that you've read the book, take it a step further. Join Linda Basso and her community in exploring the topics within *The Reluctant Marketer* in private coaching, online classes and online support groups. It's so much easier to overcome our reluctance when we are in community, rather than going it alone. Hope to see you there!

lindabasso.com/reluctantmarketer
FB: /lindabassomarketingcoach

ENDNOTES

1   Miller, Lisa PHD, *The Spiritual Child: The New Science on Parenting for Health and Lifelong Thriving* (New York: St. Martin´s press, 2016), 58, 62, 71, 75, 81.

2   White, Lawrence T. "Is Cognitive Dissonance Universal?" *Psychology Today*, Sussex Publishers, 28 June 2013, www.psychologytoday.com/blog/culture-conscious/201306/is-cognitive-dissonance-universal.

3   Newman, Kira M. "Six Ways Happiness Is Good for Your Health." Greater Good, 28 July 2015, greatergood.berkeley.edu/article/item/six_ways_happiness_is_good_for_your_health.

4   Fredrickson, Barbara, *The broaden-and-build theory of positive emotions*. (Philosophical Transactions of the Royal Society B: Biological Sciences. August 2004).

5   Guven, Cahit. "Go on, Give Society a Break and Be Happy, but Not Too Happy, Deakin Economist

Says." *Deakin University Australia*, 13 June 2011, www.deakin.edu.au/about-deakin/media-releases/articles/2011/go-on,-give-society-a-break-and-be-happy,-but-not-too-happy,-deakin-economist-says.

6 Silny, June What's So Great About Happiness, Anyway? (The Answer: Plenty!) *Happify Daily*, http://www.happify.com/hd/whats-so-great-about-happiness/

7 Fredrickson, Barbara, *The broaden-and-build theory of positive emotions.* (Philosophical Transactions of the Royal Society B: Biological Sciences. August 2004).

8 Pratt, George, and Lambrou, Peter, and Mann, John David *Code to Joy: The Four-Step Solution to Unlocking Your Natural State of Happiness* (New York: Harper Collins, 2012) 178.

9 Lewis, James R; Peterson, Jesper Aagaard, *Controversial New Religions*, (New York: Oxford University Press, 2004) 226.

10 Mosely, Glen *New Thought, Ancient Wisdom: The History and Future of the New Thought Movement* (Philadelphia, Templeton Foundation Press, 2006) 35-40

11 Pew Research Center, November 3, 2015, http://www.pewforum.org/2015/11/03/u-s-public-becoming-less-religious/

CPSIA information can be obtained
at www.ICGtesting.com
Printed in the USA
FSHW022122281018
53373FS